MW00935881

MEMORIES

A COLLECTION OF
POEMS AND ESSAYS

Tanya Hochschild

Order this book online at www.trafford.com
or email orders@trafford.com

Most Trafford titles are also available at major online book retailers.

© Copyright 2010 Tanya Hochschild.
All rights reserved. No part of this publication may be reproduced, stored in a retrieval
system, or transmitted, in any form or by any means, electronic, mechanical, photocopying,
recording, or otherwise, without the written prior permission of the author.

Printed in the United States of America.

ISBN: 978-1-4269-4334-8 (sc)
ISBN: 978-1-4269-4335-5 (ebk)

*Our mission is to efficiently provide the world's finest, most comprehensive book publishing
service, enabling every author to experience success. To find out how to publish your
book, your way, and have it available worldwide, visit us online at www.trafford.com*

Trafford rev. 09/30/2010

 www.trafford.com

North America & international
toll-free: 1 888 232 4444 (USA & Canada)
phone: 250 383 6864 ♦ fax: 812 355 4082

We think. We plan.
We think we plan.

Acknowledgments

I thank Mike Derechin for the beautiful cover photograph. My nephew Graeme Hochschild for the extraordinary animal photographs and Cathy Carroll for her in-house guidance into the mysterious capabilities of the computer. Phil Carter, for hours spent talking about the joys and difficulties of writing and Mike, my husband, for all his support.

FOR
ROY ALLAN POLONSKY

Contents

Book I

A Written Photograph

Twenty feet above, a frigate bird
holds his position in a soft wind.
His forked rudder tail sways his body,
no need to work his angled black wings.
A red pouch balloons below his fearsome beak.

I watch his unhurried tilt and flow,
"Wait!" I cry,
race away,
return camera in hand,
eager to frame his beauty.

I look up into an empty, endless sky.
He does not know waiting.

I write his photograph.

A Drop of Fog

In the Namib Desert
a mute beetle lies upside-down,
one drop of fog rolls from
its bleached spoonback
to its cupmouth, open on the sand.

Between its silence and my words
I cannot describe
what keeps it alive
except flow of life.

In this waterless place
speckled skinks sparkle,
chameleons burn black,
sidewinders scroll,
lizards leave tracks in the sand,
the bushman's newspaper.

Life is revealed in solitary lines,

Later, into the far future,
when the world floods
and property is measured in liters,
lizards will lose their feathered feet,
their second bladder,
and grow to crocodile greatness;
chameleons will move into the woods
and turn green.

Today survival depends on a drop of fog.

Lost Tribe

Baboons crouch
on an egg shaped rock,
pick fleas off each other,
hatch mayhem.
At midnight a hullabaloo,
a ballyhoo.
Screech conversations
break into grunts -
start up again.
"yoo! Yoo! YOO!"
I lie next to my husband.
We shout back at them,
"who? Who? WHO?"
slap mosquitoes
off each other.

Hunched over coffee
on canvas chairs at dawn
we watch baboons watch us;
males stony ridge faces,
babies doe eyed beauty,
young trapeze artists.
A mother croons to her infant
"aeiou." "Vowels," we say
"First lesson in language.
Next year he'll serenade us in Shakespeare."
Our laughter returned by a proud grin
from the alpha male,
whose curled fingers
strum his hairy stomach.

Treesnake in Our Driveway

Green and yellow snake
slender limb
in green and yellow tree,
your dagger head,
ready to strike.

Sinister guest, my eyes trace your body
speckled diamond scales
disappear, blend into foliage sunlight,
silky sleek.
My tree is fraught with snake.

Steady as an acrobat on a high wire,
your body sways in the breeze,
Mesmerized, I feel betrayed by the tree
who wraps you round,
gently rock-a-byes.

Your golden glinty eye appalls,
I recall Lawrence's encounter
with his snake at the water trough,
how ashamed he felt when he
threw that log.

Perhaps I could welcome you to our garden,
stroke your perfect form
drape you round my neck...
I know! I know you are lethal
slit eyed, gnarling venom,
bullet for a head...
and yet,
you look old;
down to your last skin.

Graeme@goimage.co.za

The Lion Cub

A torrent of water
the lion cub disappears
clamped between the yellow ragged jaws.
Twisting, turning, the croc tries to
tear the cub apart.

Jaws and claws wide open three lionesses
roar into the water.
Bite,
scratch,
claw the croc.
The river a frenzy of
foam
blood
snarls
the air cut by
tails
fangs
then, the water still.
The croc gone.
Lionesses with cub stagger up the bank.

Graeme@goimage.co.za

10

Tu Whit Tu Whoo

Owl, lord of darkness,
on wings fringed and velvety
screeches into the twilight pinewoods
where he waits,
master of masquerade waits,
with feathers tight
against a tall body,
ear tufts thrust upwards,
eyes narrowed,
'til a rabbit squeaks.

Owl's head,
a sound scanner,
stiff facial feathers
funnel sound to his ears.

His head bobs up and down,
huge eyes mirror his meal.
He plunges on broad wings
To the forest floor,
pierces his prey in an instant
with ice-tong talons.

My Heartbeat Echoes Their Call

Malandi kukuzi shasha na
Swerr ne kaz amfumbu
Oosisi bank manzi
E itza le maandah eh umfozi banke
Grauw tikitiki zander zonke
Lo Afrik shwe shwe
Malandi singa, malandi tinga porgonan,
We! We! Seeleni gonza "Fore!"
Evender manzi tomba
Ma shoo whew shoo
Malandi solaz
Peshu gang de manzi
Pr shik, pr shik, pr shik, phwee
Martie antvoordi

Ibises drill their song on the baked river bank
As I snooze on my chair in the shade.
Afternoon breeze blows in,
causes the river to release tears
on the croc on the bank who lies in darkness.
Africa shudders to the snap of his jaw,
Ibis tries, ibis cries for his not-so-simple life
We! We! Unheard by golfers who shout "Fore!"
The broken water swallows both.
As they sink, ibises rise, to perch on the wind.
Their wings beat,
call pr shik, pr shik to their voiceless friend.
My heartbeat
echoes their call.

The Battle of Isandlwana - Anglo Zulu War 1879

The moon slides into the glare of the sun,
an eerie eclipse, the day is done.
The Zulus come now, every one
with a loping, lolling, jog trot.
"Not a bullet to be shot!"
the young subaltern cries
grunts from the horses,
and from the men, sighs,
"Mark your target,
til you see the whites of their eyes!"

From afar they glimpse the assegais glint
the impis run at a headlong sprint.
The cooks, the grooms, the secretaries flee,
a Welsh soldier boy cries,
"Oh Woe! Oh Woe! Oh woe is me."
The brown bodies wash in like the sea,
chant their war cry, "Zee! Zee! Zee!"
The English wait with sword and gun .
Wave after wave of Zulus lunge
There are shots, and shouts and smoke and fire
bodies pile up, a funeral pyre
Others fight on like lions but fall like stones,
cairns on the veldt now protect their bones.

Whitehall never sanctioned these discords,
nor Commons nor the House of Lords.
The Zulus too did not want war
Sir Bartle Frere, an awful bore
for his own glory,
on the day of the dead moon
sent boys to death, far too soon.

The story is told by a passionate fellow,
as nanny goats graze and sheep loudly bellow
Zulus and English he knows all by name,
all still remembered, in battle the same.
After three hours his story is done
there's not a dry eye, not even one.
We whisper with him to the African air...
Salagahle —my dears, be in peace
then silently think, will war ever cease?

St. Paul's Chapel, N. Y. City

A block away from Ground Zero,
the tiny chapel,
spire barely reached
the seventh floors of the two brothers
who once towered over her.

"I will lift up mine eyes unto the hills
From whence cometh my help."

Still intact.
But now her brothers gone - struck
on that cloudless blue day.

What has happened, has happened.
We do not know what will happen next.

"My help cometh from the Lord,
Which made heaven and earth."

In the worst of times,
The best of help given
to souls suspended in silence.
Those half-alive watching over
those half-dead, comforting
the known and unknown, weeping over
the found and unfound.

"The sun shall not smite thee by day,
Nor the moon by night."

Within the white wooden interior,
grace and peace flourished where
banners,
photos,
candles,
love poems,
notes
garlands
bloomed.

Nellie Bass Durant,
from Farragut Tennessee,
embroidered a wall hanging with
the names of all the dead -
and phrases –
"there's a void in the New York skyline,
a hole as big as the one in our hearts,"

"To the 343 fire fighters who died,
Thank you New York heroes
Thank you for watching over our family."

"To New York city and all the rescuers:
Keep your spirits up. Oklahoma loves you."

"The Lord shall preserve you from all evil;
He shall preserve thy soul."

From the mangled steel and debris,
Gripping hand shovels
Gas masks
Rosaries
Face shields---
Recovery workers
with burned eyes and choked throats
came in to friendships
forged in loving arms,.
ate soups and stews cooked with care,
shoulders massaged on narrow pews
where scuff marks of heavy work boots
welcomed worshippers to services.

"The Lord is thy keeper:
The Lord is thy shade upon thy right hand."

Tables groaned under piles of
Chapsticks,
candies,
wet wipes,
Bic razors
Excedrin
Earplugs
Eyedrops.

Nothing ran out of what was being given:
love
smiles
hugs
unconditional friendship
to every race,
color,
creed
and gender.

Every house rule broken in St Paul's
Renamed now "The chaotic hotel of radical hospitality."
Podiatrists worked in the George Washington pew.
A kitchen and doctors offices were set up -
sounds of flutes and cellos filled the chapel,

But spaces still for quiet and reflection
and Waterford chandeliers to dazzle the peaceful oasis---
you could not imagine you were on earth.

"I will lift up mine eyes unto the hills,
From whence cometh my help."

Intifada

A kid in a miniskirt hops onto the bus.
Some boys call out, "Hey, come sit with us."
Pushing down the aisle, looking for a seat,
Smiles at a girl when their brown eyes meet.
Then hits her chest, as if to stop a sneeze,
And detonates a bomb hidden 'neath her chemise.
Their mothers hear the news, it doesn't take too long.
One's beyond consolation, the other's praised with song.
At the funerals the mourners chant an ancient cry,
A tooth for a tooth
An I for an I.

Tanya Hochschild

Lobsterman in Linekin Bay, Maine

The wash of water over rocks doesn't wake us.
It's the gull that cries "Hey!" at the girl
in the red bathing cap.
Later, we stand on the porch, shout "Hey!" back.
An oarsman in a row-boat looks up.

Far off sails slap, repeat on our porch.
Nearby, a lobsterman, hand over hand,
works the water, hauls his traps on board.
Like a pioneer in the old west, his ranch the sea,
the Alma Mae, old boat, his trusty horse.
He ignores other traps in vivid racing colors,
who jockey for position as the waves bring them home.

The Vineyards of Piedmont

A rooster echoes the church bells chime
in the misty Monferatto Hills.
Like vines we curl around each other
in our bed
at the Barolo Inn
and watch a russet grape leaf float
towards the earth.

The Alba Truffle Market

A divine smell leads us to the truffle market
where precious corms are carefully weighed
on jeweler's scales
and sold to chefs who shave them
over risotto and ravioli,
then wait to hear their patrons
shout, "Bravo!"

Istanbul

The waters of the Bosphorus
where Europe and Asia meet,
reflect the Dolmebache Palace
whose Baccarat balustrade glitters
lit by 4 tons of Waterford chandelier.

The waters of the Bosphorus
where Europe and Asia meet,
reflect grim faces, of heavy,
booted women, long skirts,
gray, brown and gutter green.

A Beggar in Johannesburg

He stoops on the corner of Bompas and Oxford,
a heavy sign around his neck, "Wife and five kids
to feed."
The frayed collar of his torn shirt is turned up
against the wind.
His gray stubble glints in the winter sun, his eyes
downcast.
His filthy palm catches coins dropped from half-opened
car windows.

Five days later he is in a different suburb, far from
his corner office.
The beggarmoney has bought him a swig and a swagger.
Cleaned up, he looks good in a freshly ironed shirt, shaved
and whistling.

Letter Home

We sailed into Amsterdam a week ago,
to a quay drenched in low-anchored cloud,
to walls and windows framed one to the other.

Pink and fuchsia canal houses wash
into the water, where among yachts,
they rock, swirl and sway.

How cool the climate,
how different the light from ours-
ablaze south of the burning equator.

Notice us among the café habitués.
Under the white awnings,
below the bellies of gulls.

Now, a darkening delft blue sky adds
a hot white evening star
to the palette in the harbor.

From the windows, sounds -
a crying baby, a saucepan splutter
from one a flute.

Perhaps tonight, like van Gogh,
we will see a starry, starry sky.

Relax Relax Relax

Dawn yoga class
on a lawn in India
Relax, relax, relax,

Our teacher leads us through
a synergy of energy,
guides us deeper into meditation

an ant crawls across my chin
unbearable tickle not to be relieved
relax, relax, relax,

Relax your right knee, your left knee
relax your toes, abandon all thought
fellow yogis hardly breathe

I cannot abandon all thought
achieve union with my higher self
while that ant walks on my lips

Follow your breath, hold, hold, release!
stay in the now
Relax, relax, relax,

The now is irritating
the ant's physical path
blocks my spiritual path

Go inside you where there is strength
hone the body, tone the body,
relax, relax, relax,

What if I eat the ant?
will it sting?
one lick and it is gone

The lotus-positioned yogi strikes a chime
we all come out of that deep place
except for the ant

The yogi chants, Om, Om, Om
mantra unifies body, mind and spirit,
we join in the chorus, Sh ant i, Sh ant i, Sh ant i

The Lake Palace, Udaipur, India

Troops of turbaned butlers await the barge.
doves coo Khammaghani – welcome!
From white marble ramparts,
unseen hands release red rose petals,
wafting from one heaven to another,
blessing our heads and shoulders.

Through wide doors, we escape
hot Rajasthan desert air.
The Maharana's summer palace,
jasmine garlands,
namaste greetings
soothing sitar music.

For us a brand new land,
a love affair begins,
palace, place, peace.

Gem embedded walls.
Water falls
from crystal lotus-balls.
A pigeon-wallah walks,
cracks a paddle against cloth,
scatters birds.

I pray to Ganesha, elephant-headed god
- remover of obstacles -
a stay of one thousand and one
nights under the Indian moon.
He rewards with two nights in a feather bed,
a memory forever
of Lake Pichola.

In the Streets of Old Delhi

The blare of Old Delhi,
gossip and hum,
face pressed against car window
where drift of curry, coriander
leak from labyrinth of lanes.

Gears grind in dusty potholes,
Untouchables – the honorably dirty
sweep streets, break stones,
carry basins of rocks.
Gods flash by on dashboards,
tassels bob behind overfilled auto-rickshaws,
bells chime on solitary sacred cows.

Women in shades of shocking pink saris
weave curtains of silky black hair
with hennaed hands,
exorbitant smiles blind like a lover's.

A walking zoo in Old Delhi,
mahouts ride tikka powdered painted elephants
past divinely decorated camels.
Swarms of monkeys swerve
from cobras in round baskets.
Goats prance, water buffaloes plod.

Family Patel, five on a scooter
wave as they roar by.
Bicycle rickshaws pedal past stalls
where vendors toil,
stir samosas in cast iron bowls.
Holy men, devotees, pray
to 320 million Gods,
not all at the same time.

Nobody pays attention to us fair skinned foreigners
except hungry eyes, rich in patience and hope.
They beg to be noticed;
Peck-peck the car window's glass
With bony fingers – chickens scratching for grain.

Zululand

No one warned me not to love you.
Now, after too many moves, too many homes
to drive once more down your dusty roads,
round rumps of hills
where herd boys with hard heels
wave greetings,

Lebombo wattletrees and Torchwoods
whisper welcome
in this faraway place
on the road of my youth.

Dawn lights Flametrees
which blaze back at the sun.
Buffaloes under Mkuze trees gaze
at eagles who ride the wind
over green peaceful hills,
once battlefields where history stole men.
Now renamed Kwa Zulu Natal,
the land of legends returned to Zulu dancers
foot pounding, handclapping
like crashing waves.

As wheat chaff attracts birds after harvest,
So is this place a magnet to my wandering heart -
I love it so and do not know how not to.

South Africa – Forced Removal

The children laughed as they danced
behind the bulldozer.
But when a good house crumbled
they stopped and asked,
"where will the Abrahams's sleep tonight?"

When the fig tree toppled,
they remembered the owner saying
"As long as you don't break the branches
you are welcome to come and eat."

At the museum there are photographs,
holes in the ground,
a broken vase
a torn picture of a flashy Dodge
and a proud guy in a zoot suit.
The curator says healing does take place,
but how?

St. Francis Bay lies in a bay on the Indian Ocean on the East Coast of South Africa.

A Visit Back to St. Francis Bay

At St. Francis Bay we swim to our past
in the endless sea.
With diving gannets,
red-beaked oyster catchers,
amid tumbling terns
we plumb the waters of our
children's Alma Mater.

They, now further afield,
beyond the harbouring arms of the bay
have taken with them days and nights.
Afternoon squalls still shake the tops of bushes,
send spiders on the ride of their lives,
as webs pull and tug like bungee cords,
like memories,
between branches,

In the deepening tide we hear
echoes of a dream land.
Days spent in the rain and the sun.
A wave crests and we speed back to shore,
the right place to return to.
Now as then, welcoming.

The Diamond Diggers

In the good old days
a man could kick the earth
and become wealthy.

Now rumors of "big finds"
and "lost fortunes" abound.

Entire savings gambled
on the chance
of finding the ultimate stone.

Disappointment, disillusionment,
life-stuff of
these weather-beaten people,

Living frugally in zinc-sheeted homes
along dry river beds once filled
with millions of years of diamond-bearing gravel.

Claim jumping common,
suspicion and thievery everywhere.
Cots elevated on cement filled paint cans
keeping evil spirits away at night.
Planks stored as prospective coffins.
Framed on the wall,
"What is home without Mother."

A ship, "Queen of the West" wrecked on the rocks near where a rutted sand track winds alongside the sea in South Africa. The locals named the track,

Queen of the West Boulevard

One walk on our Queen of the West Boulevard
holds us for another year.
The sun's last rays dazzle the summer folk
who play on rocks where sand and scrub meet sea
near boats, moored in driveways, open doors
where aproned women stand, and boys on boards
surf all day and into the night.

In winter sullen shuttered homes glare
as wild tides soak rocks.
A lone blue heron,
feathers pruned by the wind,
stands guard over a recently killed snake.
We range along a rutted track-
over dunes where only a Land Rover can go.
We know this place, its bush is in our blood.
One walk on our Queen of the West Boulevard
holds us for another year.

Kalk Bay Harbour – South Africa

Coloureds with calloused hands wait with quiet whites
for the fishing boats return.
Above the bay, a man on Muizenberg mountain
mirrors to the boat crews
just where the snoek swim.

The boats appear,
sunk almost to the water level,
heaving between the harbour walls.
The crowd pushes forward.
On the jetty the auction begins.
A kabeljou, seven pounds heavy is snatched.
"Fresh fish! Vars vis!" yell the fishermen.
"What am I offered for this beauty?"
"Ten bob!" calls a buyer.
A sullen look is the disdainful reply.

Children scamper between adult legs,
fisherwomen with dangerous knives
scale a fish in seconds –
watch out you don't anger them,
hope they haven't had a "dop" of the stuff
that makes them crazier than they already are.
They throw fish in separate piles, snoek, yellowtail, elf.

Holiday makers deliberate and lose
to chefs who buy and take off quickly.
Seals swim round the old wooden boats,
wait for fish carelessly flung.

In half an hour all is quiet again –
a few dogs sniff around.
The picturesque harbour still,
Tied up fishing boats bob,
a lone angler casts from the harbour wall.

Malay Fruit Seller Muizenberg Beach

"Fresh fruit! Sweet as your mother's heart,
litchees, peachies, mangoes," he chants,
"A taste of Paradise."

He tramps barefoot down the beach
khaki pants rolled to his knees,
white shirt unbuttoned to the navel.

Mom calls him over,
a pole balances on his shoulders,
baskets of fruit at either end.

He ducks under the pole,
rests the basket on the sand
a smell of sun and sugar rise.

Her red nails pinch a peach,
she points, he fills brown paper bags,
we rub the fruit in our hands, then bite.

"S,true Mom," my baby brother says,
licking juice off his fingers,
"It's as sweet as your heart."

Rio, First Grandchild

"Her name is Rio and she dances on the sand
Just like a river twists across a dusty land…"
Duran Duran

We meet, you wrapped in family
on the verge of life.
I did not know 'til then
there has always been a place
in my heart for you.
And now I know I have
been running toward you
in this race.
You, pinch of grace, small wonder -
shine on us firstborn, make us
recipients of your blessing.
So tiny, and unknowing now –
already giving so much.
You will grow into your life,
be our harvest and we
will gather together.

A Lighthouse Lullaby

A winter storm burgles
through cracks in the window;
finds itself pinned in the room.
Rain falls in paths down the thatch
pops like beads on the linoleum floor.

The lighthouse foghorn moans its vigil
The searchlight prowls our room, finds
the baby, balmy under her blanket,
with her thumb in her mouth
all plugged in for sleep.

Grandparents Preparing for Children's Visit

I think I have things ready for the arrival of Janet and Co (other than the crib which a friend is lending me.) I went to Publix, CVS, Baileys and Jerry's to find all the things on Jane's list. Babies are not us. In addition, Janet has shipped in a special seat that Baby Cara prefers at this time, and a breast pump. We have a high chair, a bike chair, a thing that you pull behind a bike, a beach stroller, a booster seat, a seat for the bath, a seat that serves as a high chair in restaurants, a musical mobile and a sheet set of Teddy Bear bedding. The teddies wear red scarves and are at a picnic. David tells me he is looking forward to the visit even though at this time, his office, "the baby's room," is chocabloc with baby paraphernalia and he cannot get near his desk.

Jazz Mama Daydream

You the yes in yesterday
You my jazz mama come what may
Your curvaceous lips and feet
Movin' dancin' to the beat
All day long the records play
Til late at nite you bob and sway
piano tonks, jazz fills the air
Dad says "go to bed" - makes it clear
Mama's answer drowned a tenor sax
"Ah just let the kid relax."
So we floated through our years
On Benny, Basie and Ella's tears
Later doggin' around clubs and bars
Sittin' in the garden under stars
The 'ol moon travellin' cross the sky
And I thought you would never die.

Now, cut loose, I'm tired and sore
The music faint, you don't j jump no more.
But, in my dreams I hear the notes
See you smile through memories motes
We hum Desafinado through which we glide
Then I no longer seek and I no longer hide.

Mummy

You at your mahogany dressing-table,
misty behind the curling smoke of your ciggie
tilted, in the red glass ashtray.
Your tongue slicks your lips which you cover
with a pointy red crayon, with a tissue
blot off the excess.
You smile at me, beautiful mother
dressed for another
boring medical dinner.
How can you stand those disinfected small
wives, whose tight white lips perpetually
purse, whose noses sniff scandal,
who never turn cartwheels in the garden,
or win the Mother's race on sportsday,
or drive the tennis team to Farouk's
Ice Cream Emporium, win or lose?
You choose some rouge, pat it on your cheeks
clip golden hoops, on each ear,
open your powder-puff, dab the tip of your nose.
You shake out your hair, I stare at
your reflection in three angled mirrors, perfect
profiles and familiar face.
You swivel round, adjust your broderie anglaise blouse
Slip your arched feet into sandals, softly sing
"The sheik of Araby"
I call out, "Your heart belongs to me,"
We shout out the song, then you nod.
I pick up the perfume bottle, you offer your neck.
Three short sharp sprays, you are ready to leave.
You lean down to kiss me goodnight,
"don't let the bedbugs…"

45

Rosh Hashonah

Before leaving for the sanctuary
father blesses us.
His cool surgeon's hands settle
above my forehead.
"May the Lord Bless and Keep you
in Health for another year."
He stops time.
I half turn my head,
see baby brother nibble crumbs
off the stained lace cloth
where he spilt his once-a-year sip
of Manischewitz wine.

Dad's hands weigh my head down,
guide my gaze to the Persian carpet,
to carved legs of the polished mahogany sideboard,
to Spotty's nose resting
on my shiny black
patent leather shoes.

Those Summer Sundays

Six days a week,
suited and tied to his medical practice,
father labored with patients
pregnant with expectations,
who interrupted
our homework, dinners, sports matches
to call him away.
They say he was the most respected surgeon .

But those summer Sundays he is our Dad,
no longer shy.
During his weekly swim,
his spectacles and watch
left on the folded towel.

On the pool steps
looking towards the deep end,
hands in prayer position
elbows raised at right angles
he prepares for the dive.

My brothers and I scatter to far parts of the pool.
A deep breath, he bends his knees,
launches
always to land with a loud belly flop,
spray shoots from his body.
Shortsighted he peers at us, smiles
then, with windmill arms, splashing legs
he gains the deep end, where he pauses, turns.

With squeals of delight we follow him
buffeted by his wake.
He clambers out, dries himself,
replaces watch, and spectacles,

Father walks away.

Conversations During a Tropical Storm

"I WILL BE A LONG TIME DEAD!"
his mother always told us.
Now as she fights to live,
the sodden grass sings a reply
to the incontinent gutter
as midnight downpour sweeps
across our roof.
The old dog groans
an answer to thunder's rumbles,
curls into himself.

All night water sinks into the ground,
the wind bangs a shutter which I latch.
Rain soaks my arm.
I hear her well used retort,
"YOU WON'T MELT!"
Is she pounding on our porch
Or is it just the storm?
Outside I imagine her dip and dance
Between heaven and earth.

Intrepid mother, platoon sergeant
during the war.
Ran a swimming school
(like a platoon sergeant)
during peacetime.
Taught "tadpoles" – her word for beginners,
to blow bubbles in a basin.
Proudly declared when talk turned to domesticity,
"I CANNOT BOIL AN EGG."

A flash of lightening charges through the room
as the telephone begins to ring.
Before we answer to hear sad news,
I recall her at rugby games
exhorting the players to,
"MOVE YOUR BLOODY ARSE!"

Haikus

Look! Baby squirrel!
calls out city girl with joy
at streaking chipmunk.

The golfer walked by
the alligator as he
chomped gopher tortoise.

Thirsty grey cat drank
pink minute maid lemonade
from a round blue plate.

Loss of a mother
birth of a first granddaughter
Two bookends of life.

Spa – a place of peace
no galloping wildebeest
just welcome gnus.

Morning storm attacks
gathering army of clouds
volleys of thunder.

RENGA
His belly unfilled
I've collared the cormorant
his taken fish mine.

He stands in the falling rain
drenched angel with sodden wings.

51

Sanibel Haikus

Dressed for moon landing
mosquito buzzes gardener
can't find firm purchase

Golden eye of duck
so its all in the details
and spotting them well

Every atom is us
we are mysterious pond
we are waves and leaves

Here comes grasshopper
bent knee, bronze chest, coiled back legs
one triumphant leap

The sun beats down now
raccoons rest in leafy tree
watching you and me.

Crane curses osprey
steals flapping fish from him
stolen from ibis

When season nears end
snowbirds give huge food parties
to clean out their fridge

Locals however
enjoy two-for-one coupons
at area Eats.

Tryst on Bowman's beach
dawn wedding ceremony
witnessed by turtles.

Scared by hurricanes
Pete moves back to Milwaukee
blizzard hits next day.

Dunes golfer curses
when tenth ball finds the water
from the second tee.

Betty Ray surprised
to see her golf ball holed
up in osprey's nest.

Ted's drive is perfect
black crow swoops down picks up ball
Ted loses one stroke.

A Sonnet for a Sanibel Summer

Ding is just darling at this time of year
mosquitoes aren't bad, of them have no fear
ballets by fish who leap from the water
gators who prowl each mile and a quarter
Leaping lizards! Of which there are plenty
Despite being meals for avian gentry
The mangoes hang heavy upon the trees
To test if they're ripe, just give them a squeeze

Music's a second language on this isle
Especially in summer – listen a while
We enjoy front row seats on our lanai
Of the tree frog concert from palms nearby
So if it's all the same to you my dear
We'd like to stay for many a year.

Scrabble on Saturday Morning

As soft rain falls
we play Scrabble on the lanai
in the cooler temperature.
We set up the board,
keep our eyes shut, feel for lucky letters.

Water eases off the roof,
washes palm fronds,
fills bromeliads.
It's been a long, dry spell.

I study the seven letters before me.
Enjoying the rain, I think of "drench", "quench",
but a "q," "u," "d" and "h" are needed.
How to use the letters?

Beyond the rain soaked garden
ducks head into the river,
seven downy babies bounce
in the windblown waves.
Coming up close behind the papyrus
like a floating coffin
an alligator swerves, pauses
and swerves again.

Mama clucks her babies back to shore.
I rearrange the letters,
"menaces" appears.
Fifty point bonus! What a way to start
the game.
Like the ducks, we are off and running.

A Pileated Woodpecker Raps Jazz

Early one morning here's what I heard
No Charlie Parker but a real yardbird

Thump thump thump on utility pole,
plays his instrument, he's got soul,

Drill that baby, rock the hood.
You're on the wood.

On the street is where he entertains
turtles, ibises and sandhill cranes,

His musical range, the whole nine
doin' fine, rocks it, rocks it line by line.

Taps out what he's seen, where he's been,
an avian icon moves like a cyclone.

He plunges, lunges, quite the syncopator,
dips, then rips, stirs an alligator.

Goes so fast this can't last.
Beak of the bird, blurred.

You're a jazzler
a hep razzle dazzler!

A circuit breaker
a true volt maker.

Drum your red head
get out the lead.

Notch notes on the timber
make Mamma want to rumba.

Cuts wood, chips away, he's able,
three step turn, hops up on the cable,

Plays it fast, beaky, bluesy,
pole – box – wire - bird's not choosy.

His love song tumbles down,
a jazz affair all over town.

Music's floatin' along the street.
He's got an improv man truly beat.

Motown mogul for a moment.
I'm in melodic foment.

Cat's got the spirit, he's really movin',
Got to me, now I'm groovin'.

When he's done, had his fun
when he's thru, played it true

Sweet Woody Woodpecker gives me the eye,
waves his wings, shoots for the sky.

I run on in the morning streets
jogged by the rhythm of that bad bird's beats.

Graffrigeriti

This is just to say

Do not eat
the plums
in the box
on the second shelf

I'm saving them
for the dinner party
Thursday night
something sweet and cold

Forgive me
but I am not
driving over the bridge
again to Costco.

This is just to say

The blonde in our bed
Is me
Henri suggested
a change

Tried to stay up
to see your reaction
but a day at a spa
is so tiring.

Running Away with the Spoon

I wonder as I walk, why a silver spoon
is lying on the side of the road?
Has it had enough of living in the mansion?
Did it jump out of the picnic basket
and through the open window
as the Jag pulled out of the driveway?
Perhaps the spoon wants to see
what living on the wild side is like.
And the people who use the spoon,
to sip consommé
or slice crème brulée, what of them?
Do they miss the spoon
or just use another, out of the pantry drawer?
walk on, into a poorer neighborhood,
where, in the gutter, I see a plastic fork.
Why are people throwing cutlery away?
Something is going on.
The spoon, one of the smart set,
feels her life is empty, wants more.
Meets a fork with the soul of a poet
who can turn her Monday morning
into a Saturday night.
As kids, we learned
the dish ran away with the spoon.
But these are modern times…
so perhaps a tryst, near the corner of 4th and Vine?
"Where I'll meet ya hon – and make ya mine."
I turn for home and when I pass them both again
a thought, I'd be over the moon
if all their hopes and dreams come true.

Across the street a little dog laughed.

Rodeo Night

Buckaroos earn an 8 second livin'
ridin' bulls named Hanky Panky,
Bullocity and Robin.

Bullridin's ain't for sissies.
Jake, Clay, Travis or Buckshot'll
splain to you,

"Climbin' aboard a bull
clingin' to his back like burdock,
ain't no stention of ranch work.

When we splode thru the chute,
Snorty's a freight train.
Best bail out, kiss the bull goodbye."

Buckshot sucks back, sighs,
"Think on it…Bull's 2000 pounds with horn
Cowboy's 160 pounds with hat."

Chaparral Charlie whips back,
waves an arm at the universe,
boots bull round arena,

Bull humps, twists,
bucks cowboy into the air
like popcorn from a hot skillet.

The salty victor digs dirt as Charlie
tumbles like a weed for the rails, his
star-spangled bandanna floatin' loose.

The Pianist – A Prose Poem

At last night's piano recital a hush fell over the auditorium. Miss Growpling appeared from right of stage, attired in a black evening dress, a small red brooch near her collar. She had sparse sandy hair, her complexion sallow in a frail frame. She had repopularised Carl Nielson, one of the greatest Danish composers.

She approached the Baldwin Concert Grand, bowed to the audience and settled on the bench, embraced by the chandelier's orange glow. It was as if honey was rising from the hive.

Her hands, rather huge for a woman, I thought, launched directly into the agitated first movement. The G key in the third octave stuck during the raging storm section.

The artist's temperament, sorely affected, not by embarrassment but by anger - became scherzophrenic. She commenced to tear the piano apart with fierce hammering on the keys. Strings stretched beyond their limit, keys rubbed against their neighbors, some became loose, other keys hung on. The ivories took the worst punishment from Miss G's noisy knuckle syndrome. The C, two octaves below middle C cowered with A at the bottom of the keyboard. In the inner wilderness of wood and wire, havoc reigned. Piano wires snapped, jack springs dislodged, wood chips flew. The audience ducked and swerved to avoid debris flying off the piano. An E flat major landed near the front row. The pedal groaned. It was certainly depressed.

The audience gasped as they saw the front leg of the piano buckle slightly inward, jarred by the racing, pacing fingers of the performer. The screws stripped and ran, followed by hinges, castors, locks and rods. The piano began to list and fall.

Awakening to the last movement which began slow and measured, I noticed the ivories had taken up their places on the board. Miss Growpling, lovely in person and musicianship, caressed, and cajoled joy from the keys. The appreciative audience called for encores and the evening ended in general rejoicing.

Season of Poets

April - season of poets
when birds fly in,
sing among burst of saplings.
When movement ripples grass,
tortoises - pigeon-toed, lime green, gold
roam from winter shelter.

Humming wind windmills willow fronds
at water's edge of dams and ponds,
a steady rain brings flow again,
in April.

From under frozen wood,
a gathering of words,
once burrowed, now bob
in a pool of memory,
poetic elegance to be walked out
as a barefoot poem.

Making a Poem

A woodpecker taps on the shutter
wearing his beak to a stump,
making a home, much like I make a poem;
tap it out, the rhythm and rhyme,
struggle to sing through words
printed on paper, home for a hope - a hunch.
It's not as if words rush forward like wild white ponies
on a sweep of beach, unstoppable.
Like the shutter, poems are hard to penetrate.
Like the woodpecker I tap tap tap until
one still soft evening
the wild ponies graze, the bird is quiet, the words come -
not from me,
but through me.
Making a poem is like praying,
singing,
loving,
living.
The delight of not knowing where it ends.
The relief of a beginning begun.

Thinking about Breaking Down Writer's Block

Doors close, too many locks, where are the keys?
I have the tools of mood, memory and emotion,
a box full of metaphor, simile and alliterations
Yet what should be a festival of form lies tattered, forlorn.

'

If you don't have a process, you can't have a product.
No reflex, no song,
The ever climbing shadow of doubt
Is active in its darkness
and I can't see
a sonnet in me.
I can't even see a word.

I want to make words of my feelings
As I rush down the road.
But without cogs and wheels I have lost my bearings.
I cannot drive forward or backward to memory.
Cannot release the brake called thought.

Emily Dickinson wrote

This is my letter to the world
That never wrote to Me —
The simple News that Nature told — with tender Majesty

Her Message is committed
To Hands I cannot see —
For love of Her — Sweet — countrymen —
Judge tenderly — of Me

Held Mail

Replies arrive eventually
From Ladies with parasols –
Sauntering Gentlemen with Canes
and little Girls with Dolls.

They ink the pallid stationary
As twere a bright bouquet –
Alas Em now drifted deep
Cannot read what they say.

The letters bend many an ear
They weigh with written load –
bees, trees – hum their tune
fill late Dickinson's abode.

From Mumbai – on the hill
From London – sodden in the Fog
After her everlasting fashion
New York replies –from Blog

Now libraries in town collect
Letters folded in Amherst
Judges and Professors all
Adjust – and do their worst.

Annual Check-Up

The doctor's fingers pause on my breast,
retrace and pause again.
"I feel," she frowns, "a mass, a nodule,
something's here."
I take a direct hit to my gut.
Feel alive at that moment - my own extinction.
I go from having it all to a haze of crumpled memories.
Outside I hail a cab in the frenzied noise of midtown
"Where to?" he asks
"Where to?" I echo, looking down at my blouse's
stripes, closer than prison bars.

Baggage

Oh
to pack my old baggage
in a suitcase.
To
ride unclaimed
on
the carousel,
while
I take off.

Together

I track my life down the trail we tread.
I am the wildness
in the park of your imagination.
You claimed me, tamed me.
All this time, half of me is you;
we become each other.

But,
sometimes,
when you are the wilderness
and I feel stones between us
I want all of myself again.

Survival of the Fittest

Darwin sailed to the Galapagos,
legendary land in lapis,
linked the chain of life
which clung in the balance,
called his idea: origin of the species.
Selected into the life boat, he wrote,
are those who adapt.

Naturally we selected each other.
To inhabit your world I needed
like the flightless cormorant,
to clip my wings.
To inhabit my world you needed,
like a Galapagos sea lion,
stones to grind in your stomach
to digest life with a wife.

Both born under fire signs,
we evolved from volcanic eruptions.
You learned, like the Galapagos dove
to coo your appreciation,
I learned not to be your albatross
on Saturday rugby afternoons.

Like Sally Lightfoot crabs we scampered
through years of precious life,
found footholds on earth
nurtured our young,
comical as boobies with blue flippered feet,
they squeaked and danced,
appealing to us to keep feeding them.

Two ancients,
once with dominant genes, now recessive,
slow as tortoises in ill-fitting leather coats,
We bubble,
crawl,
grip,
glare and stare -live in harmony,
going forward.

To Do List

You remove
I curve
You bend
I suspend
You hold
I fold

You hook and hinge
I unlock and open
We
roll
rotate
weave
flow
grasp
tighten

Rush down a chute towards the sea
to accompanying sounds of celebration

You release
I dismantle
We are done.

Scissorcide

I walk into another salon
hopes high, the Maestro
will get it right this time.
He asks how I would like it?
"Something chic that I can shake
When I step out of the shower."

Sure, he smiles, wields his scissors,
Then a frown - problem with my frizzes?
He lifts a lock and lets it drop
his voice drips with disdain,
As he fingers my mane.
"I dunno who cut your hair," he snips
"but they've …" he leaves the sentence,
like my ego, undone.

Up north my hair played the game
It swung, it shone, it was tame.
I used to leave it well alone,
It had tone.
But here, in humid temperature, it soars unchecked,
bedecks my head
with snarls and clumps.
Feels dead.

My bathroom drawer, filled with The Cream,
vanilla bean, an exotic bottle of
balsama suavizador – and plenty more,
some fiber wax guaranteed to make hair relax
but as it's wont, my hair remains a hairdon't.
A soothing balm, some gel, some goop
But still my coif goes for a loop.
No clip, no comb, no foam can help
This wet lank mop that looks like kelp

There remain some spas and bars
urban and retro, suburban and metro,
I haven't stepped foot into yet.
But, I must admit
I'm a hairbreadth away from buying a hat
And that'll be that!

Cocktail Napkins

According to decorator extraordinaire
Dot Draper, a great party
doesn't require expensive food or a well trained staff.
All you need, she says in her latest book,
is a hostess who expects to have a good time,
and clever touches that give your home a party feeling.

She can't help you if you don't have a party feeling,
even though she is a decorator extraordinaire.
Blame yourself if you don't have a good time;
but promise if you're glum, don't be a party
pooper and be left out of the A team's black book,
because its lonely at home even with 5 on your staff.

Consider the cocktail napkin; don't stay home and starve
…embroidered doilies of yore with the homey feeling
are gone, replaced by designs that fill a book;
there are bumblebees, whimsical fish, tres extraordinaire,
according to Dot the hors d'oeuvres at your party
will be flattened in no time!

She says it twice, "I tell you in no time, no time
flat." By the latest, say eightish, the waitstaff
are gone, sideplates and glasses drying post-party,
revelers full of booze and pate are feeling
no pain, as they disappear, walk on air
for tis the season, next week's party is already booked.

Dot has verve, just read her book.
"Entertaining is Fun" she's been known for some time
as the doyenne of how to make silk from a sow's ear.
She's au fait with the group who walk with a staff,
use napkins of linen, rather silken in feeling.
Are seen at the White House, when they have a party.

Don't think Democrat or Republican party,
Not only Texans have their names in W's book
He expands to all his lovin' feelin'
then it's gone, gone, gone for all time.
W don' know jack about his staff!
The French finds it quite extraordinaire.
The stuff of napkins filled a book,
gave readers a good feeling if they took the time.
It is quite extraordinaire what Dot brought to the party.

A Shy Shiite and the Painting at the Frick

At the museum on Saturday
I saw an astonishing sight.
In front of a painting of Shropshire sheep
stood an unshaven, shy, Shiite.

"I settled in Shropshire once," he whispered
"'cos my passion is shepherding sheep."
I chose not to answer, felt the man was a chancer,
Then I swear I saw one sheep leap.

"You saw that too? Did you? Did you?"
He told me meekly, he visits here weekly,
Just to stand and speak to the sheep.
"They dance for me, specialize in shim-sham,
They're really good – Allah Kazam!"
"Are you saying the sheep tap?!"
"Exactly, old chap!"

Then as if on cue, except for a few,
The sheep did a fancy routine.
With a 5-6-7-8
The flock did not hesitate –
They brush pulled to the right
Jumped high in flight
In response to musical notations
Of four beat combinations,
Hops and jumps from heel to toe,
This was no do-si-do.
With a shuffle and a slide,
Chug, riff and glide,
Dancin' the stomp, the rush, the brush –

"HUSH!"
The guard stood there.
Silence! There is to be no noise in here!
The Shiite, like a Dervish, whirled away
but I, no, no, I chose to stay.
In the painting sheep stood stock still,
across the river and up the hill.
Not a shiver, not a quiver.
I saw the Shiite through the window
He turned to look at me and smile
Then he disappeared down museum mile.

A Road Show in Tinseltown

ROLL CAMERAS! ACTION!

The fast, furious, almost famous,
the wanna-be-a star trek to the city,
speed through locale in downtown L.A.
to Hollywood Boulevard exit.
Biker Boyz, bros on fire, trailed by cast of thousands
cross dotted line in pursuit of a dream.
Bob, Carol, Ted and Alice,
Uptight shot of wardrobe crew
in yellow van.
They see coming attraction
from rear window; but are so not into it -
being on union time.
Billy Wildest (it's all about the extras in L.A.)
yells at camera man,
"Focus!
Close up!
Return to background!
Highlight palms!
Want Greed,
Ambition,
Love,
Vanity.
Need Sound! Track sound,
soundtrack – cut!"

Pan-out flyover, flashback of a man and woman
in blue van, both bankable stars
having an affair to remember;
going all the way round the bend,
Billy, maestro of film noir, in the dark,
unaware his movie reel spools real life.
Now the wrap.
Later an Oscar nomination
for this movie shot in one location.
A thousand words when they take best picture
at THE ceremony, where industry
guys and dolls show footage and cleavage,
promise not to speak from here to eternity.

THE END.

This Suds for You

Duds in suds' future is bright, fresh clean
women applaudin' from Tulsa to New Orleans.
Seems laundry's movin' from basement to heights,
They're all in the party - darks, delicates, lights.

News from Whirlpool: "Laundry's gettin' an upstairs room."
Hear Mrs. Beeton shout Va Va Voom!
Folks at Maytag need no convincin'
woman's job is washin', ironin', rinsin'.

The dryer and the washer
are gonna get much posher.
Dry cleanin' unit, sink for soakin' clothes-
Banish forever those washaday woes.

"Will this really help?" you may well ask.
Oh yes! it's the Zen of an everyday task.
Think of it as a peaceful, meditative time.
Hear water swirl as it vanishes grime.
It's not a just rumor
the female consumer,
launders seven to nine hours a week.
A fact to make Ms. Greer and Ms. Steinem freak.

Powders and softeners have moved from best to bester,
Delightin' the bachelor girl and the empty nester.
Products like laundry fragrances and ironin' sprays
have been ramped up so as to garner our praise.

While we're havin' fun in our new 'Wash Center',
Husbands' noses are gettin' just a tad benter,
But you men out there, don't disparage
Whirlpool's introducin', "The future of the garage!"

Mrs. Benz' Roadtrip

On the morning of August 12, 1888
Bertha Benz woke early, her husband, slept late

She and her two sons, Richard and Oigin,
pushed down the road her husband's motorvagen.

Without losing any time
they sped off to the town of Pforzheim.
Startling people along the way
scaring them witless, that is to say.

Bertha was 39 when she made this trip without
too much bother,
her motive she said was to visit her mother.

But in truth the reason she was all for it
was to convince the public to buy after they saw it!

The three drove along in the motorized carriage
Bertha and the boys, products of her marriage,

This was not part of any workshop trials,
they aimed to drive the 106 miles.

Bertha knew her car well,
Steered it capably through dale and dell

Along the way they did require
one of her garters to insulate a wire.

She unblocked a fuel pipe with a hairpin,
(this gal had moxie) took it all on the chin.

A cobbler replaced leather linings on the brake,
away they went with a shimmy and a shake.

A blacksmith mended a broken chain,
said of his work, "Och, I could do zis again and
again!"

After 12 hours they reached their destination hale
and hearty,
immediately after the welcome party

she sent a telegram to Mr. Benz, who told all his
friends,
this wife of mine recommends

another gear – this gives me the thrills –
to overcome difficulties – she says, driving up
hills.

And that is the story of Mrs. Bertha Benz
there's no more to say, this is where it ends.

Technology Blues

I sit in front of the computer,
with a bowl of cereal, open up email.
The street empty
except for an early morning jogger
when suddenly, a crowd appear on the screen.
All because…
I gave out my email address to a company
who sold it to the devil in cyberspace.

Harry and David fob off fruit,
Williams Sonoma puts me in a coma
with all the pots he offers.
L.L. Bean, Marshalls and Sak's caterwaul - and that's not all.
Abercrombie and Kent implore
a visit to another foreign shore.
I do like hearing from Victoria
in her padded push-up bra, - but careful what you tell her,
she shares her secrets. I don't even have lipstick on
but with Victoria in the room I feel fully dressed.
Ralph Lauren daily appears,
in his short sleeve black polo shirt,
he's been visiting for years.
Jackson and Perkins bring flowering gifts galore,
Barnes and Noble's stories fill many a bookstore.
What the hell! Here come Harry and David once more.
And although I am feeling perfectly fine,
Dr. Weil is about to reveal a medical goldmine,
his daily hint on how to stay well.
I hit the delete button, they whoosh away,
Guess what? They're here to stay, back the next day!

And let's not even discuss the phone
where strangers call you by your first name;
I tell you folks – it's a crying shame!!

I hardly shop with a catalogue,
nevermind facebook, myspace, twitter or blog.
This new communication thing leaves me in a fog.
With words Roget could not foresee.
I'm sticking with Webster's dictionary.

A Handful of Summers – two sonnets

Tennis 1970

Sungold girls
Ball swirls
Tumbling hair
Laughter share
Game won
Great fun
Shade tree
Drink tea

Slim limbs
Laze loose
Freckled arms
Youthful charms
Silken hands
Wedding bands

Tennis 40 years on

Sunblocked dames
Two set games
No rush
Hot flush
Bandaged knees
Throaty wheeze
Boiled milk skin
Hardly thin

Forgotten score
Joints sore
Massage thighs
Winded sighs
Upperarms flap
Timeout! Nap.

Reunion 10-19-04

Here we are, a lifetime away from girlhood
meeting in a shrunken school.
Memories ripe enough to pick
tumble through forty years,
land in spaces between things altered on our bodies.

Again the dawdle and giggle of girls
sharing lovelust memories of Miss Thornton-Thomas,
Didi, Sexy, Biffy, Noo-Noo, and Heebie-Jeebie
our pony-tailed heads huddled together,
tortured about who is a virgin, who has the curse.
We slept like lozenges, woke effervescent in the morning.

Now, in the safe anchorage of the dorm,
the five of us (as we always did) drift to the window.
The pink ribbon tied between our beds
in an adolescent ceremony, links us still.
Sexy, once a sketch of a girl
answers now to Carolyn.
(It is rumored she had an affair with Norman Mailer.)
She lies arm flung back
womanly breasts where buds began.

Didi - Christine - sits on the end of a bed,
watches us, as always saying nothing.
Captain of Tennis; remember the swank of her serve?
Biffy, first in Math, her wiry hair now straightened,
Private gym instructors, surgeons,
an annual trip to an ashram in India -
her salon-tanned body is AMAZING–ly orange!

The women overflow the hard, thin beds.
Half of them are their younger selves.
They sleep, voices repeat Madame's
"je suis, tu es, il est, elle est, nous sommes, vous etes"
Noo-Noo shouts out in her sleep, "All for One!"
pierces other dreams; Heebie Jeebie responds "And one for All!"
They curl, unfurl, sleep like the girls they will always be
until the last bell rings.

Mirrors Ain't What They Used To Be

I peer at the reflection,
blink to see who's there.
Lost is the Miss of the past.
A cast of familiar strangers peer back.
I glimpse my brother and my father, Jack.
Same nose but not quite.
The eyes of my mother, same wrinkles between.
The longer I stare I see my face change,
rearrange itself,
with long dark hair,
no lines around my mouth…

This face ain't me.
How can it be?
I'm thirty three
busy driving kids to school
to soccer practice to ballet
with a quick stop at the supermarket
buy tonight's dinner.
But wait! Back then I was thinner,
Who is this dame in my mirror?
She with those flaws bedecked.
Not me! Not the last time I checked.

Mirrors do not reflect the me
of ideas, feelings and memory,
so I blink again. Aha! I see
a grandmother, aunt and wife
realize gratefully this is my life,
the here and now, my finest hour
a time of power, a true reflection,
not one lost in the myth of the past,
what can you say?
I've grown up - at last!

Who I Would Be If I Weren't Who I Am

In my kitchen, I cook up the woman I would be if I weren't who I am. Ingredients need to be at their prime. This is a full bodied nourishing dish, usually served as the main course on a bed of lettuce. A local, aged vintage is the suggested accompaniment.

Ingredients
Margaret Mead's mind
Bridget Bardot's body
Navratilova's forearm
Annike's backswing,
Erica Jong for obvious reasons.
A pinch of Susan Butcher mushing to Nome
A dab of Beryl Markham flying west with the night
The voice of Maria
The drama of Sarah (careful she's hot – don't burn)

Method

Slowly melt. Ignore any hiss or crackle. When tender, bring to
boiling point but on no account boil. This dish is ruined by
boiling. In a separate bowl whisk together and sprinkle into pot,
essence of
Mandela,
Mother Teresa
Mother Goose
Gandhi
From the shelf shake a teaspoon's full, of
once upon a thyme
rhythm of Fats
quack of ugly duckling
Add a dash – oh wotthehell - a whole line of Edna St. Vincent
Millay. "What lips my lips have kissed."

Keep covered. Serve hot. Bon Appétit.

DAD, MOM, ERIC, TANYA, ROY 1949

Book II

Roy 1960

Mom drives us home from shopping in Rosebank as Chubby Checker belts out "C'mon Baby, Let's do the Twist," on Springbok Radio's Top Ten hits of the week. Eric sits next to her in the passenger seat of her black Austin. Roy and I are stuck to the vinyl of the backseat. The news comes on and the announcer talks about the summer's heat and drought. Crops have failed, farmers are no longer hiring and many black farm workers are walking to the cities hoping to find jobs. Mom draws her hand across her forehead. The air coming through the open windows is not cooling us down at all.

Roy suddenly leans forward and says,

"Ma, he's reading my mind!"

"Who's reading your mind Roy?" Mom asks wearily, watching the traffic ahead of her.

Roy points to the radio, "He is!" he almost shouts. "Please Ma, switch him off!"

"It's the radio, Mom," Eric says puzzled "Roy says it's the man on the radio."

She turns the dial and after it clicks off there is silence in the car. Mom looks at Roy in the rear view mirror, "O.K.?" she asks.

He nods, puts his head down. I am alarmed; what does Roy mean? Is he joking? Perhaps he just wants silence. It is hot, we are tired.

At the roadside, Africans sit on the emerald Kikuyu grass, under flowering Jacaranda trees, near the walls and fences of their white employees' homes. They meet regularly during their off hours from their domestic jobs. Among the group are cooks in caps and aprons; gardeners in overalls, women, some with babies on their backs. As we slow to turn right into Central Street, the uninhibited laughter of an African newspaper-seller fills the car. Whites do not usually laugh in public like that, perhaps they are too inhibited by colonial upbringing: an explosion from the belly of utter joy. I cannot help smiling, turn to see if Roy is enjoying this moment. He is not. At home we help Mom carry parcels into the house, stumbling around the dogs who are jumping on us in a frenzy of welcome. "Roychie! How about a swim?" He loves swimming; we all do, and spend every spare summer moment in the pool. I barely hear him say, "No Tan," as he trudges upstairs to his room.

A few days later Roy refuses to come down for dinner, when our Grandmother is visiting. "She will read my mind." I look at my mother, she looks as confused as I feel. He refuses to go to school. He keeps saying he hears voices in his head.

He had turned thirteen a few short months before, had read his Bar Mitzvah portion ably and enthusiastically, surrounded by his loyal group of friends, all of them looking like penguins in their suits and ties. Roy is athletic, he is on the soccer team and excels at golf, he entertains us playing jazz on the piano, looks sharp as a pin in his neat school uniform, dark hair brushed back, always smiling, a popular boy, with no indication of any storm clouds in his life. He is always first out of the door when the liftclub (carpool) arrives. Now he is suspicious of everyone. My parents make an appointment to see a Professor of Psychiatry, a personal friend. Mom repeats to Eric and me some of their conversation.

"He asked us if there was any history of mental illness in our family. Dad replied, 'Certainly not!'" Mom told him, not that she knows of.

Dad believes there has been a chemical disturbance in Roy's brain, probably brought on by puberty.

Roy is interviewed, examined and subjected to many tests. The diagnosis is schizophrenia; electro-shock therapy, the protocol.

I am horrified that electro-shock treatment is going to scramble Roy's fine brain. I have no grounds to know this is so, just a gut feeling it is too drastic a treatment. I don't understand what is happening to Roy and why, why out of the blue this should happen? He had no symptoms until that day he said he felt the man on the radio was reading his mind. Now he is anxious, isolated, hears voices, has hallucinations and doesn't want to see his friends, doesn't want to go to school. I can't talk to Dad about Roy, he just starts crying. Eric clams up and seems irritated. Mom goes on trying to make all of our lives enjoyable. I don't know if she has spoken to Gran. At school I tell my three best friends, Kathy, Didi and Wynne. We hold each other and cry. They have known Roy for years. I wonder if they will stop coming over to visit.

We drift through the days, our house as silent as a morgue. The servants continue their cleaning and cooking routine, but there is no whistling and humming and calling to each other.

How could Roy have disappeared overnight? I have lost my sibling to something I cannot understand. Roy, my young, sweet brother has gone. The person in his place is neither frightening nor dangerous. He still says, "Please" and "Thank you" but he sits looking at us, his coal-black eyes fearful. Sometimes he smiles, his private joke, sometimes holds his head in both his hands, as if he were trying to squeeze the life out of it.

At the dinner table, Dad doesn't turn on the radio anymore to listen to the evening news, something he always did before Roy became ill. Mom has told him voices on the radio upset Roy. Dad moves more inside himself than ever; buries himself in his work. Our meals are silent. Our family grief is not discussed. Phineas serves and takes off the plates, often touching Roy's shoulder and saying, "Oh Roychie, you enjoyed the chicken tonight," or, "See Madam, Roychie ate all his spinach, champion Roy." Roy looks at Phineas, neither smiling nor frowning.

The servants are all so gentle and kind to Roy, endlessly patient. They seem to know how to be with him. They have a reservoir of goodwill, not only limited to Roy; it extends to all of us. One night, after dinner, I sit with Evalina and the other servants in the yard talking about Roy, her "white son" as she calls him and whom she has known since he was a baby. "Every night, before hamba lala, go to sleep, it was me singing to him." The others sit with their eyes down, slowly shaking their heads. She carried him wrapped in a blanket on her back as she worked in the house, bathed him and fed him. We talk about lives and what it all means. Mostly I talk, trying to find meaning. They listen, Mabel sucks gravy off her fingers, while Phineas sips tea from a tin mug.

Evalina has her arm around me. She says, "Everyone deserves a life, every human being." She clicks her tongue against the back of her top teeth as if trying to find a clue as to what we can do.

The others nod and murmur in agreement.

I look at each of these caring, dignified, intelligent people, whose lives, because they are black, are so proscribed by the government's laws, whose physical movements and opportunities are so limited, whose future is written in their passbooks.

Evalina turns to the others and says, "Maybe ukuthwasa, ne?" They look at her and seem to be thinking about what she has just said.

"What did you say Evie, what does that word mean?"

"It means Roy might have a healing sickness," she tells me. "In our culture the ancestors call you to be a healer, a sangoma, but first you seem very sick …you hear the voices, you behave strange…"

"Dad will never go for that," I say.

"Talk to him, tell him," she replies.

I know Dad will not be sympathetic to a Xhosa belief, steeped as he is in Western medicine. Once, when I told him I had booked a reflexology appointment, an alternative method of healing, he had said, "Well Tanya, there are many ways to waste your money." A few days later when I brought up the subject of ukuthwasa, he looked at me as if I was speaking in tongues, then he told me he knew nothing about that and it could not be as effective as he and Mom were hoping for, by following the Professor of Psychiatry's recommendations.

Eric and I take turns driving with Mom when she takes Roy for electroshock treatment to Sanatoria, where he stays overnight. No other options are suggested. Two attendants meet our car and hustle Roy out. Mom and I drive down the long, straight driveway of the sanatorium, away from the building, toward the gates. She looks in the rear view mirror, begins to brake.

I turn to see what she sees.

Roy chases the car, the attendants dressed in white gaining on him.

"Drive Mom! Drive! He's better off here!"

She gasps, pushes her foot down on the accelerator. We shoot through the gates, weep as we drive through the suburbs back home.

Dad is still at work when we reach home. Mom paces through the house, walks to a chair, sits down, immediately gets up, walks into her bedroom, lies down, but is already swinging her legs onto the floor. She paces back downstairs. Eric and I feel helpless as she keeps going from room to room, unable to find calm. I worry that I too will suddenly hear voices in my head. Why shouldn't it happen to me, or Eric, just like it happened to Roy?

Dad and I go for walks. He cries when we talk about Roy; I never see him cry in front of Mom. He also goes on and on about the boy I marry. He must have good health he insists. He doesn't think much of the crowd I hang around with. I do. I don't tell him Robert Davis has proposed and wants us to run away together. I tell Eric, he is flabbergasted. I tell him not to worry, it is not going to happen.

Dad arranges through his medical connections for the attendants to pick Roy up, saving Mom the grueling journey. They arrive, are quietly shown into Roy's room. We hear his surprised shouts throughout the house. "No! No! Mom, please don't let them take me!"

We sit imprisoned in the living room until he is quiet. Perhaps they drug him with an injection. I don't want to see if he is in a strait jacket. After the front door closes there is a silence louder than Roy's frantic shouts.

We hear a soft knock at the living room door. "Tea, Madam." Mabel carries before her ample bosom a tray holding a teapot, cups and saucers, a sugar bowl and a jug of milk. "Have some sweet tea. It is good for you." Mabel the cook is a grandmotherly type, about to retire, and she takes charge in the best way she knows how.

She soon returns with another tray of home baked scones with strawberry jam and whipped cream.

ROY circa 1960

1960 (Later)

The life of the family shifts. Roy's condition displaces us all. It is a strain everyday to accommodate Roy, to put him at ease, to be patient. We falter, try to find a stable perch. My world, spent half at home, half at school presents a solution. I ask to be a boarder for the two remaining years of high school. My parents agree.

When, however, Mom and I say goodbye in her car outside Roedean school gates – my trunk already placed at the end of my bed in the dormitory - I say to her,

"I feel like a rat leaving a sinking ship."

"Not at all," she replies, "You are not to think like that. We'll be alright."

"Ma, I promise you, Roy will always be in my life." I mean it. I have a lifetime commitment. I feel lousy about leaving but we are still in the same city, a short car drive away.

"I know darling."

We hug each other.

"And don't forget, I know something you don't."

"What?" I murmur, afraid to ask.

"I know how to get around the school's rules. I was here too, you know. Also, I'll be one of the mothers driving your hockey and tennis teams to 'away' games. We'll see each other lots more than this short visiting list allows."

The bell rings. Suddenly the quadrangle is filled with noisy schoolgirls.

"C'mon!" a group of friends call to me.

"Go!" she smiles.

The first night in the dormitory, the Matron, grey haired Miss Biggs, a spinster who has made the school her world, stands at the door,

"Now girls, go quickly and quietly to bed."

Ten voices respond as we climb into the narrow beds, "Good night Madam."

She flicks off the light and we hear her sensible lace-up shoes clomp down the wooden corridor.

Sarah Henwood, three beds down the line, is reading under the sheets. Suddenly the dormitory is flooded with light. Biggsy has crept back quietly. She glares, pauses, then hisses,

"Sarah! Reading is NOT allowed after lights out."

"But Madam, I was not reading!" replies Sarah who has kicked the flashlight to the end of her bed, where it is now casting an eerie beam through the light sheet and thin blanket.

"What is that light in your bed?" demands the stern Matron.

Sarah dives under the sheets, comes back up with a huge grin, "Oh Madam, it's my torch, I've been looking for it for days!"

I laugh with the others and it feels good. It also feels safe here at school.

The days are filled with poetry, history, science and geography, sport and homework, friendships and laughter, but when I think about Roy and what is going on at home I feel a deep sadness, wondering if he will ever get better, if our family will ever get better.

During the holidays a boyfriend and I pick Roy up from a talking session with a psychiatrist.

Back in the car, Roy, who is amazingly lucid at times, says "You know he is madder than I am."

We laugh, the doctor's idiosyncrasies are well-known.

My parents decide to travel with Roy to Cheadle, in Cheshire, England, where R.D. Laing is having success with schizophrenia. They fly home after two weeks, leaving him, as they tell us, "in good hands."

After Roy has been in England a year, a friend of the family telephones from London to say she has met Roy wandering around Trafalgar Square not knowing where he is. My parents fly to bring him back. For many years my mother insists he live at home. She never complains, never raises her voice to him, he is once again part of our family. Mom and he have a standing golf game every Saturday morning. He is still a terrific golfer and enjoys playing. The caddies and Roy know each other. After golf he and Mom sit on the verandah and enjoy the club's specialty drink, Cola tonic and lemonade. Mom bears his illness with fortitude and an uncomplaining grace.

1947

"You have a baby brother!" Granny tells Eric and me, who are hanging around waiting for her to put the phone down. He and I take off from her house where we have been brought to wait for this news. Our grandparents live five blocks from our home. We run through the open front door, past the Ali Baba pots, taller than us, down the driveway, followed by Granny's black house-maid shouting, "Stop, children, Stop!"

We run down 7th Avenue, past the Leigh's house, past the Schwartz'. Past the Grunhut's, nearer we run to busy Central Street, where we live. I look back to the elderly woman in her white eyelet apron, and matching eyelet cap. She's reached the Leigh's house, just passing their orange brick wall. She bends over, her hands on her knees, breathing deeply to catch her breath. I look ahead where Eric runs, not looking back. He, is four years old, a year older than me. I chase after him and the distance widens between us and the maid. Soon she is a distant figure, shouting, "Oh God! Please stop children, oh God!"

God is on our side. We don't get run over crossing Central Street. We race passed the Culliner's, the Fourie's and the Joseph's, then turn into our driveway, dash through the garage door into the yard, through the kitchen, down the hall, up the stairs, across the landing into our parents' bedroom. Mom is in bed, holding a sleeping baby with jet black hair. She smiles. "This is your brother, Roy Allan." We stand with my father at the foot of the oak bed looking at him. It is December 2, 1947.

Our home is in the tree-lined Lower Houghton suburb of Johannesburg. Dad is a gynecologist and obstetrician. Mom is a housewife and Captain of her golf club. Evalina Msomi is our nanny. We don't know Mabel our cook's last name or Phineas, the gardener. He also works in the house in the early mornings, polishing and vacuuming. A night watchman patrols the property. Betty, an elderly washerwoman, comes on Mondays to work in the outside laundry. We also have a procession of dogs. Spotty lives a long life, but most of the dogs get run over on Central Street.

Our childhood days unfold without drama, cocooned as we are. Our friends live in similar homes, some with swimming pools and tennis courts. Our days are spent Monday to Friday being driven to and from school, by a carpool, shared by neighborhood mothers. We take for granted driving through huge gates, past manicured gardens, waiting at enormous front doors, greeting young mothers in beautiful clothes. Smiling gardeners and maids wave the car hello and goodbye.

Johannesburg's fabulous weather allows us to play outdoors from early morning to last thing at night. Even in the middle of winter, noon is hot.

Afternoon sports change with the seasons; swimming in the summer - playing tennis, soccer or cricket all year around.

There is always food on the table, and courteous manners. If we leave food on the plate, a parent might remark, "Eat up, children are starving in Europe." I never make the connection that if I eat two lamb chops instead of three why that makes any difference to a child in far away Europe.

Tea is served at eleven in the morning and again at four in the afternoon. On weekends the afternoon tea is something to look forward to, because that is when our parents come downstairs again from their zizz, (afternoon nap) and we no longer have to stay quiet.

Our parents never raise their voices to one another. I wonder if it is because the servants are always around and watching, and they, as the employers have to appear exemplary. The thought crosses my mind some pretentious neighbors, who dress their waiters in fezes and red sashes over their white uniforms, are so

Impressed with their own self importance, they don't understand that fate, not necessarily merit, played a role in their being born white and middle class in apartheid South Africa, and therefore The Boss. My brothers and I say they think they pee eau de cologne.

1950's
Esther – Zulu Chef

The noise from the kitchen is louder than usual. We're in the dining-room finishing breakfast before leaving for school. Dad has already left for work. Suddenly, a blood-curdling scream and shouts in Zulu. My mother rushes from the room, down the passage toward the open kitchen door, shouting back at us, "Stay where you are!" The outside kitchen door to the yard slams. We hear running feet, dogs barking, another door slams, more running feet. My mother's voice shouts, "Esther, put that knife down!" I half stand up, am pulled back by Eric, "Mom says to stay here!" We listen, the sounds are further away. Phineas, our gardener, runs past the dining room window.

"What do you think is going on?" asks Roy.

Nobody answers him. We all get up, go toward the kitchen. Looking down the passage we see a crazed Esther, eyes wild. Her hand high above her head holds a butcher knife. Her other hand clenches the night watchman's coat collar. The night watchman's room is behind the aviary, next to the golf course. We hardly know him and only see him when we come back from family meals or movies late at night. He sits near the gate in the driveway in a huge brown army coat around a brazier his knobkierie (fighting stick) held in his hand.

A black man I've never seen before, one of many who probably spend the night in the servants' yard illegally, is talking quietly in Zulu. Mom is standing close by, saying, "Please Esther, listen to him." It seems an age before the knife is lowered, then removed by the man. The night watchman adjusts his collar, walks out of the kitchen towards his room.

We run back to the dining-room and are sitting like angels when my mother reappears.

"What happened Ma?"

"The night watchman complained Esther had not given him enough porridge and that it was cold. She became annoyed."

Later, when we come home from school, Esther's room has been cleared out.

Evalina, our nanny, tells us, "Mummy gave her a very good reference and said the next Madam can phone her, so she can tell her Esther is a good cook."

"Yes," says Roy, "But Mummy mustn't say how good she is with a knife!"

Evalina – Xhosa Nanny

Our nanny, Evalina's bed takes up three-quarters of her room. Its four legs are on bricks so the tokoloshe can't jump on her when she's sleeping and slit her throat. We believe in the tokoloshe, a hairy dwarf-like creature, sent by bad spirits, usually at night, to cause illness, injury and even death. Evie has told me he only spooks black people. Why? I ask. Because she says, white people don't believe in him, so he's got no power over them.

She lifts me onto her bed, because it's too high for me to climb onto. I sit on her embroidered cover and watch her rubbing cream into her face.

"Why do you do that?"

"Because it makes my skin lighter," she answers.

I tell her, I lie by the pool to get darker, and she laughs. We sing the chorus of the popular Jeremy Taylor song, "Tell me, tell me why, I want to know the facts, why all the black people want to go white and the white people want to go black." Evie is my second mother, my third parent.

On her wall she has a picture of Sir Seretse Khama, the black King of Bechuanaland, and his white, English wife Ruth. She loves the picture, tells me Bechuanaland is on our northern border, how Sir Seretse is so clever he went to England to attend Oxford University, then he met Ruth Williams, a clerk, and married her. Theirs is called a mixed marriage Evie tells me. When I ask her if there are any mixed marriages in South Africa, she says one word in three words, A part heid, that mean two words apart hate. She explains further, "Immorality Act – it's illegal." I nod, as if I understand.

"You know," she says," it is against the law for a white person to love a black person, or a black person to love a white person."

"But I love you Evie," I say.

"Oh darling," she laughs, "and I love you."

We are in her room one day when the radio beeps three times and then ends with one long beep. It's the One o' clock news. The stern voice of the announcer reports that a notorious black gang , the Msomi Gang, is terrorizing the township. I know Evelina's last name is Msomi, a Xhosa last name. I tell her I can keep a secret and ask her if she's related to the Msomi Gang. Tears of laughter fill her eyes, she slaps her black knees. I notice her legs are brown, but her knees are black and she takes me and rocks me backwards and forwards repeating, "No! No!"

Evie's favorite song is The Tennessee Waltz. She sings it to me all the time, very soft and very slow,

"I was dancin' with my darlin' to the Tennessee Waltz..."

Evie's darling is Roderick, a driver for a company in Johannesburg. I always hope the police won't raid whenever Roderick sleeps over. Evie's little room became very crowded when Eric, named after my elder brother, is born. Evie carries him, wrapped in a blanket on her back as she works in our house. He sleeps with his head against her back. We love him.

One morning Esther, the cook who sleeps in the room next to Evalina, comes to my mother, they talk quietly and my mother follows her to the servants' yard, telling us not to come. Eric had died during the night.

Later I knock on Evie's door but there is no answer. It is only a few weeks later Roderick is killed in a car crash.

My mother phones a black taxi company, who drive Evie to Park Station, where she takes a train to a town near her kraal.

"We have given her leave and she will come back when she feels better," my mother explains to us.

"But she didn't say goodbye," I cry.

"Because it's not goodbye," Mom answers.

"I want to write to her," I insist.

"Oh darling, I don't have an address for Evie."

I sit with Spotty, my fox terrier in the garden. Evie knows everything about me, the way I eat my soft-boiled egg, then turn the empty egg over so the unbroken shell is on the top and pretend I haven't touched it, how I say the multiplication tables, my favorite shirt… I don't even know where she lives. Softly I begin to hum, "I was dancin' with my darlin'…"

Phineas –Sotho Gardener

Phineas teaches us a verse he has learned at the Mission School,
   "It's advisable to hamba (get going)
   When you stumble on a mamba
   For if you do not tshetsha (hurry up)
   You'll expire on a stretcher."

We sing this as we dig. Mom has given us a section of the rockery to plant whatever we like and we like cactus. Phineas explains to us cactus don't drink. We understand he means we mustn't water them too much. He is helping us as he clips the hedge and talks to the next door gardener, who is working nearby. Spotty, our fox-terrier, lies on the hot grass, smiling in his sleep. We find snails and shongololos. We show Phineas and he puts one on his arm. We watch the centipede's one thousand feet walk up Phineas' arm. Then he gently replaces him in the soil.

September arrives. It is Spring, time to get the swimming pool ready for the long summer months. Eric, Roy and I follow Phineas, down the moss covered steps into the empty swimming pool. We are wearing long rubber boots, bought for rainstorms, perfect for this job. We are going to help Phineas scrub down the pool, empty of water during the winter months. A slick green slime has grown along the floor and walls. We have hard brushes, which we dip into the bucket filled with a chlorine based mixture Phineas has made; this is the smell of summer. We swipe the brushes up and down the walls and the floors, alternatively dipping them into the bucket. I think we are more in the way than helpful, but Phineas smiles, has endless patience with us, and goes over the areas we have already worked on. When he is satisfied all the green slime has gone, he asks us to turn the hose on. We drag the hose to the deep end and open it full blast. A commotion of African ibises watch us from their perches on the willow trees.

The next morning I wake excited to see how deep the pool is, how much water has filled the pool during the night. I run downstairs and outside to the pool, disappointed to see it is only a foot deep in the deep end and still dry in the shallow end. Later that day we paddle. Each morning it is deeper until one day it is filled and we dive in, swim a length underwater. Phineas adds chemicals to the water every few days. He works for a long time, skimming the pool for stray leaves. He keeps it in sparkling condition.

We are in the pool all summer long, after our homework is done, sometimes late into the night, after we have waited a half hour after supper for the food to be digested. Otherwise, we are told in stern voices, we will cramp and drown.

"Get out NOW!" adults command towards bedtime, but we always manage one more length, then shivering skitter indoors, up the stairs, dive into the warm tub, which Evalina has filled.

On Sunday afternoons Dad "swims". He places his watch next to his spectacles on a folded towel, then he stands on the steps for what seems a very long time. He looks toward the deep end, arranges his hands in a prayer position, elbows at right angles to the ground. This is our signal to get out of the way of the launch. We scatter to different parts of the pool. He bends his knees, takes a huge breath, more like a snort, projects himself forward and every time smacks the water in a loud belly flop. Spray shoots away from his body. He begins his swim to the deep end, his style never ceasing to amuse all of us. With snorts and turns of his head to the left and then the right, but never in the water, he exhales through both his nose and his mouth, his arms meanwhile doing a wild windmill. Somehow with splashing legs and his upward body movement, he slowly gains distance and eventually reaches the other side. There he pauses before making his way back, in the same manner. He clambers out, towels himself dry, straps his watch to his wrist, hooks his spectacles behind his ears and that is his swim for the week.

Mom prefers to lie on a chaise under the jacaranda tree at the side of the pool. Bing Crosby's honeyed voice floats towards her from the gramophone in our study, as she keeps her eye on us. Sometimes, before I swim, I straddle her, sit on her flat stomach, watch her draw her red lips around the white cigarette. Lazy smoke drifts toward the hot sky. Her long wavy hair falls onto her shoulders and the elastic peasant blouse moves up and down as she breathes. She is a fun, beautiful mother and plays with us endlessly. She loves walking on her hands, her curvy tanned legs straight up, toes pointed. My brothers and I copy her, but she always stays upside down the longest. We are clumsy compared to her. Sometimes she holds our feet and she tells us to walk on our hands. We walk forward while she steps back, holding our feet. In that way we get a feeling of how it should feel, balanced and steady. After she lets go, we totter on our hands for a short space before collapsing on the lawn or diving back in the pool.

Night-Night

We each have our own bedroom, Eric's looks the top lawn and Central Street. Roy's overlooks the swimming pool and mine has a balcony and I can see Killarney Golf Course from beyond the bottom lawn. Mom and Dad's bedroom is in a separate wing. I love my room with the white wicker furniture, and especially the mosquito net which during the day is wound up into a huge ball above the bed, but at night it drapes around the bed and it is like being in a fairy castle. But it doesn't protect me from the Ironman. The Ironman comes plodding slowly towards me many nights. It all begins with me noticing the leaves on the trees across the golf course gently beginning to move. Then I see him – he is in no hurry, he crosses the concrete drainage ditch, crosses the fifteenth fairway, plods through the tall grass of the rough, swings his iron arms over the fence until his huge iron legs are on the grass of our bottom lawn. I lie unable to move. He reaches the house, climbs the wall and is now on the balcony outside my bedroom. He rattles the burglar bars on the windows and sticks his square iron head into the room. I wake up screaming. Dad comes through. "Is it the Ironman again?" he asks. "Yes!" I cry. He sits on my bed with the light on and tells me it is just a bad dream. He waits until I lie back down and fall asleep.

Dad has a busy night life. If he isn't being called out to deliver a baby, or with me after an Ironman visit, he is waking me, even when I am six years old to sit on the potty. Sometimes he is too late, I have already wet the bed. He lifts me up, dresses me in dry pajamas, and changes the sheets. I sit curled up half asleep in the arm chair. Then he lifts me up again, tucks me into bed and kisses me goodnight. He never once complains, he is never impatient

123

and he never makes me feel bad. I feel bad anyway and I ask him when he thinks I will stop. He replies, "You are perfectly fine." Then he says what becomes a mantra all through our lives, "Be well and happy." Finally he says, "you will outgrow this phase." He is right. I do.

Johannesburg

Dad works so hard he doesn't spend much time with us. I tell him the bank is overflowing with his money, he doesn't think that's so funny. I don't mean to be funny. I want him to spend more time with us and not always in his suit and tie. He tries. On Sundays he invites me to go on his rounds with him to visit new-born babies and their mothers. He practices at the Florence Nightingale, Joubert Park Nursing Home and the Marymount. He loves history and won a lot of prizes when he was in school for being a very good history scholar. One day after we finish with his rounds, he tells me we are not going straight home, as usual. He is going to give me a history lesson about Johannesburg.

"Johannesburg dates from the year 1886," Dad tells me "Today, we will drive down some significant streets so you will understand Johannesburg began as a gold mining camp."

We drive west along Main Reef Road, which people say is the richest road in the world. As if Dad reads my thoughts, he says,

"We are driving on top of the world's richest gold reef. It is more than sixty miles long. On a farm near here the first prospector stumbled upon a gold bearing reef."

"Wow!" I say, warming to the romantic story of gold, "The farmer was lucky to be able to sell mining rights to the prospectors."

"On the contrary," my father explains, "for farmers, wealth lies on the surface. The land provides them with crops. It also feeds their cattle. No, they were reluctant to sell, and don't forget, these people were Voortrekker stock, suspicious of the English."

I wait for an exciting climax, the Eureka moment, but Dad's story is painfully slow and he loses my attention. I roll up the window as grit blows from the mine dumps; gets in my teeth. Mine dumps dominate the landscape south of Johannesburg. They are mountains made from waste brought up from tunnels, deep in the earth, where the gold is mined. They look soft and inviting, shining in the sunlight like yellow beach sand.

"Do you know how Johannesburg got its name?"

"No," I answer and pray that he makes it short. He does.

"Well, eventually there were so many claims and so many prospectors that two government men, Johannes Joubert and Johan Rissik, formed a commission to decide which farms would be proclaimed for mining, and where the best site of a village was to be, to accommodate the growing numbers of men. They chose the site of Johannesburg because it was roughly in the center of the line of claims. You know the English equivalent of the name Johan?"

"John," I answer.

"Yes. These two men report the findings of their commission to Paul Kruger, the President, and suggest to him the town be called Johannesburg. He agrees, especially after they add, "Your Honor's name is also Johannes.""

Dad says at the present time three hundred thousand black migrant workers make up the labor force on the mines. They live in compounds, each tribe separate because tribal warfare often breaks out. They travel from Swaziland, Temboland, Nyasaland, Basutoland, Bechuanaland, Zululand, and areas way north. The black tribesmen are all drawn to eGoli, the city of gold. Bachelors come to earn lobola, bride-price, which they give to the father of the girl they want to marry.

"What about men who are already married, what about their wives and children?"

"The wives stay home to look after the crops and the cattle."

"Dad, how do they understand each other, if they all come from different tribes?" Fanagalo, he tells me, is the lingua franca on the mines, a mixture of English, Afrikaans and different black languages.

"I know some fanagalo," I say, "Esther often talks to me like that, 'Hau, umfaan! hamba out of my kishen, now-now sies wena!' She mixes up languages when she tells me to get out of her kitchen."

We drive to visit a friend of my father's who owns a concession store on one of the mine compounds. It is a magic place, Swazi blankets hang overhead, one wall is stacked with trunks. There are gramophones, guitars, penny whistles, mouth organs, watches, dresses for women and girls, shirts and overcoats, gentlemen's hats with orange feathers in them. Cooking pots and tins are everywhere, as are trinkets, candles, matches, cigarettes, umbrellas and shoes. The most interesting medicinal plants are under the glass counter. These are parts of animal skins, roots, powders, dried up plants, the sought after "muti" (medicine) from home, which the rural miners believe are powerful beyond white man's medicine, and can heal any disease or fulfill any wish. Certain roots bring back estranged lovers, others help you get a wife. The counter contains spells and charms. Three miners shop together. They pore over what looks to me like dust in a bottle. They talk in quiet voices. The older black man helping them behind the counter notices me, asks if there is something I need. I shake my head from side to side and he turns his attention back to the trio. Between the three of them they come up with the money and leave with the bottle of dust.

"What was that?" I ask him.

"It is for men to use, and not for children to know," he answers sternly and walks away. Twelve years old is no longer a child I think to myself. I stay at this counter looking at different colored powders, gluey clumps, lion fat?, (I have heard black men smear it on for courage), I want to know more and tell myself to remember to come back when I am older.

Back in the city we stop in Simmonds Street, where Dad tells me chains were strung, and in between the chains was Johannesburg's first unofficial stock exchange.

Mom's father, our Grandpa Morris, is a stockbroker. I have been to the balcony of the Johannesburg Stock Exchange with our family. It was something to do with a new issue Grandpa was involved in. Granny stood with us in hat and gloves, "proud as Punch" looking down on the trading floor. Grandpa stood to one side talking to other men in suits. There was a lot of activity, men shouted, waved papers, others on step-ladders changed numbers. I don't know how they knew what's going on. A bell rang and all noise suddenly stopped. The men on the balcony shook hands, the ladies kissed. Granny invited everyone home to their house for drinks. It was some house. Even then we knew it was grand. It stood on a huge city block, surrounded by a thick white wall. The architect, J.A. Hoogterp, was famous for his Dutch gabled homes and "Noordhoek" was a fine example of his work.

Dad and I drive down Quartz Street, Claim Street and Nugget Street, now in the metropolis of Hillbrow, a neighbourhood near downtown Johannesburg. He tells me about the excitement surrounding the discovery of the gold fields. He mentions the leaders of the industry, Sir Lionel Phillips, the Albu family, P.M. Anderson, the Oppenheimers, and others.

He tells me about the treatment of miner's phthisis (silicosis), cyanide poisoning and pneumonia as we park outside the South African Institute for Medical Research built by the Transvaal Chamber of Mines. I feel privileged to listen to him as he talks. His interest in and knowledge of medicine holds my attention.

"In the early days, the miners suffered and died from hazards of working so deep underground. Many mines adopted better sanitation, nursing services, and when it was seen there was a reduction in the death rate of the miners, many other mines adopted these procedures."

Often we feel tremors and are reminded Johannesburg is still a mining town. Many homes in Johburg, as we call it, are built on undermined ground. Often, I think of what is going on thousands of feet below my bed. I imagine miners working in long dark passages, their boots in water, their headlamps helping them find gold bearing rock. When the shaking stops after we feel a tremor I pray the miners have had time to get to safety. Sinkholes appear unexpectedly. A house, the family fast asleep, disappeared one night. The morning's paper carries a picture of a deep hole and people standing near the rim, looking down.

"Gold is the lifeblood of Johannesburg, of this country. We are far and away the world's largest producer of gold, with immense reserves." Dad says. We turn for home, drive through aristocratic suburbs, where mining magnates lived, their homes hidden by high walls, over which clouds of pink bougainvillea cascade. Our route takes us curving down Munro Drive from where we see the treed northern suburbs, the purple Magaliesberg Mountains beyond. It's very exciting to think we are driving over the biggest factory in the world, thousands of feet below us.

Heights

Eric, Roy and I have a compulsion to court danger from high places. We play a game where we jump from the second storey stairway onto the ceiling of a broom cupboard tucked into the curve of the stairs way below, then race back upstairs to wait for a chance to do it again. One time I take off, fly through the air and land on the target which caves in. I fall through into the darkness below. Eric and Roy's eyes are huge as they peer over the banister way above me. I, sprawl on a vacuum cleaner; look up unhurt, through the splintered thin wooden ceiling of the broom cupboard. Disturbed dust and feathers from the feather duster float above my head.

Another favorite jump is from the flat roof of the night watchman's room, which is at the edge of our property, far from the house, bordering on the rough of the golf course. To get onto the roof we climb the thick trunk of an old willow tree, heft ourselves from branch to branch, until eventually we grab enough fronds to swing ourselves onto the roof. The jump is onto a grassy hill next to the borehole, which supplies us with water from deep down in the ground. I know how to fall well, and run well, which is what we have to do, because often we are chased by the irate night watchman, who we wake up with our savage yells as we leap off the roof.

One day I land hard and my arm goes right through the thick Kikuyu grass into the earth and into a vat of something wet and pungent. We have discovered a cache of skokiaan, African moonshine, a home-brewed concoction made from almost anything that rots; brown bread, yeast, Fastmove (a cane spirit) fermented fruit. The Zulus call it Mbamba. To bamba somebody, means to hit them. Many fights are blamed on "too much pousa"-drink. Wilson, normally quiet and hardworking, the gardener from next door, sometimes comes lurching up the driveway, eyes crocodile-red, calling for Esther, our enormous Zulu cook. She stands looking at him, arms on her ample hips, shouting, "Aikona!! Hamba wena! Go home, you babelas, drunken man with your crocodile eyes, too much bloody pousa!" Blacks, or Bantu, as they were then called, are forbidden to drink liquor. The Liquor Squad drives around looking for skokiaan, which they pour onto the ground.

We decide not to tell our parents but we are really scared and cover the evidence as best we can. The shebeen Queen or King in our neighborhood would be furious to know they had been discovered. We immediately stop the game and keep away from that part of the property.

The only time I knock myself out is not on a planned fall. I am high up in the leathery green branches of the loquat tree on a Saturday afternoon. My brothers are down the road playing cricket, our parents are taking their week-end "zizz." (afternoon nap.) The custard yellow oval fruit hang everywhere and it is easy to sit on one branch and pluck it off the stems. I suck the creamy sweet pulp off the smooth nut; swallow the skin, spit out the nuts, the size of small chestnuts. I am often up this tree during the short loquat season, after coming home from school. From this perch I spy on our next door neighbor, Harrow Brenner, a University of Witwatersrand student, whom I'm in love with.

I come to in Phineas', our gardener's arms, as he carries me upstairs to my parents.

"I find Miss Tannie lying in the rockery." They put me in my mother's bed but not before forbidding me to climb the loquat tree again. Fat chance!

Police Raid

One night we're woken up by banging on the servants' doors in the yard. Our parents are out and my brothers and I peep between the slats of the venetian blinds in an upstairs bedroom and hear a policeman shout, "Gooi die vette uit!" which we know is Afrikaans for "Throw the fat one out." Esther comes flying out the door, in her see through nightie, her one arm trying to shield her breasts. We have seen raids before.

"Please let no-one be visiting here illegally tonight" I whisper.

"Another bloody police raid," Eric whispers back.

Roy says, "Are they going to be arrested? Are they going to jail?"

"No, I'm sure their passbooks are in order. Just let's hope none of their friends are staying over tonight," I answer.

"I hate when the police raid," Roy says.

"It's the law," Eric says, "the bloody stupid law."

Esther, Evalina and Phineas, all in their pajamas, stand barefoot in the cold yard. The policemen search their rooms, we see the light of their flashlights dancing around the walls. I have never seen Esther without her doek on, covering her head. Her hair is springy around her face. She looks different from when she works in the kitchen. After a while the black policemen come out of the three rooms, all shaking their heads. The white policeman who has been standing in the yard says,

"O.K. gaan slaap, you mense, daar's niks hier, O.K. go to sleep, there's nothing here."

We hear their van start up and stop further up the road. The neigbourhood dogs bark. Phineas, Evalina and Esther stand talking in the yard. Esther is cross, she keeps clicking her tongue and shaking her head. Phineas takes deep breaths as if he had just run a mile and Evalina stands with her head down. I see her wipe a tear from her eyes.

The next morning I tell my parents what had happened to Evalina and the others. Mom goes to talk to them but I am not allowed in the kitchen when they have their meeting. Afterwards our family talks about pass raids.

"Dad, why do they do that to blacks, whites don't have to carry passbooks on them all the time?"

"They want to control the number of blacks living in the cities," he answers.

"Wouldn't you get so angry if you left your pass in one suit pocket, and the police stopped you and you got arrested and sent to jail?"

"Yes."

"And without that bloody book, you can't get married, can't buy a house, even if you are in Johburg and you don't have a book, they say you are not in Johburg, because you don't have a book that says where you are." says Eric.

"It's so bloody confusing and unfair," I say.

Afternoons

We spend many afternoons running with our dogs on the bottom lawn of our property. The late afternoon summer sun streams between the branches of the willow trees, which grow on our side of the fence between us and the 14th hole of Killarney golf course.

Beyond the fence the tall thatch grass is a favorite playground of my brothers and our friends. We occupy this rough as part of our property, and have cut a hole in the fence. Often we tie the top of the thatch together creating tepees, under which we sit, unseen by passing golfers.

One day a young, thin caddy, walks up the fairway, head down, pushing against the back of a giant of a man. The man leans back, his full weight falls into the youngster's hands. They form a triangle, the fat white man leaning back and the young thin caddy leaning forward his arms outstretched supporting the white man's lower back. Another caddy, labors under the weight of an oversize golf bag. Snatches of their conversation reach us,

"Faga lo stim!" (Hurry up!) the caddy carrying the bag yells to his friend.

The other boy laughs and answers, "Ebaba mafuta, mina hamba!" (This father is fat, I'm coming.)

We are mesmerized by this scene, cannot believe what we are seeing. "Look," says Roy, "his tummy is leading the charge!"

His tummy certainly is the biggest we had ever seen. As we watch, it jiggles up the fairway, hardly contained by a patterned shirt which is stretched to breaking point. He wears bright long pants, unlike the usual golfer's long shorts and long socks up to their knees. On his head is a straw boater, so we can't see much of his face. As the trio moves away, we fall about laughing. Afterwards, we enact the scene over and over for our nanny and mother, exchanging roles of caddies and golfers. Both women roar with laughter and clap their hands at our pantomime. Mom tells us she hears about this man in the Club's golf shop. He is an American; that in itself is exciting news for us – our very first sight of an American. Mom says he is used to driving a golf cart - unheard of in South Africa - so he negotiated to hire the young caddy to push him for eighteen holes.

His name, she tells us, is Spyros P. Skouros, and he is in town to see Johnny Schlesinger, the movie magnate - something about the film industry. We love the sound and rhythm of his name. At school, for days after, when I come across my brothers in the playground or walking along the corridor, one of us shouts out "SPYROS!" and waits to hear the return call, "P. SKOUROS!"

Another day I am swinging on the willow branches overhanging the golf course when the dogs begin to bark and run frantically up and down the chain-link fence. I run to them and see a black man crouching about ten feet away in the long grass. He glares at me.

"What are you doing!" I yell above the barking of the dogs.

"Shitting," the hapless man replies.

That word shocks me. I have never heard anybody use it before, not even the rough gang at school. His father obviously has never asked him, as ours does in a stiff, medical tone, "Did your bowels move this morning?" He is not swearing. He does not intend offense.

I pull the dogs away by their collars and run back to the house, my head spinning with all sorts of thoughts: Should I run back to him with a toilet roll and throw it over the fence? Should I ask Phineas, to invite him to use the servant's toilet? I feel ashamed when I think of the three bathrooms in our house and one in the servant's quarters. I feel sorry for him and I resent him for embarrassing me.

In the end I do nothing.

The High Holy Days

The Jewish New Year, Rosh Hashonah, is a busy time as we prepare for the joyous feast. Esther and Evalina, sit outside in the sun, their legs straight before them, polishing the silver. My brothers and I bathe Spotty, our Fox Terrier, in a zinc tub near them. He hates it, afterwards goes nose first into a long skid across the lawn, then rolls over and over, stands up, shakes himself. Some of the spray hits Esther. She yells, "Take that bloody dog away!"

Everything in the house is made shiny. We are excited to wear our new clothes. In front of each place setting on the lace tablecloth are bowls filled with apples and honey for a sweet year. There are bowls of nuts, dried fruits and candy. Mom arranges Sweetheart roses in the center of the table. She lights the candles, recites the prayer. After blessing the wine, Dad takes the first sip, then passes the silver goblet around the table and we all take a sip. Roy, the youngest in the family leans his head way back, preparing to drain all the wine. Mom says, "Not so much!" and then more urgently, "That's enough!" Dad blesses the round challah, the braided sweet bread, breaks it and passes portions to each of us. We begin our meal with chicken soup and matzo balls, then a roast leg of lamb and vegetables. We all say Esther really knows how to roast potatoes, crunchy on the outside, soft inside. The meal ends with Granny's famous chocolate mousse.

Before leaving for Shul we stand before Dad. He places his hands on each of our heads in turn, blesses us, asks God to look after us and give us a healthy year. We drive to Wolmarans Street Shul, where Mom and I sit with the other women upstairs, separated from the men. I put on a pious face, watch Mervin Kessler, a boy from school, who sits directly below with his father and brother. A sea of men, their shoulders covered by tallit (prayer shawls), their heads covered with hats or yalmulkes, sway and murmur as they follow the service. Mom also puts on her pious face, sits quietly throughout the service. She looks at the Torah, but I think she is remembering her golf game, not like the lady sitting next to her who is reading aloud in Hebrew, while rocking back and forth. The Rabbi's sermons always seem to be about fire and brimstone but I enjoy the sweet voices of the choir, hidden behind a curtain. Dad and his brothers, sit in the front row, near the bimah, with their faces in the prayer books.

On the ride home I notice the stars seem brighter than on any other night, Johannesburg feels peaceful. Preparing for bed, I brush my teeth, looking out the window at the Milky Way. I try to imagine God, the universe and my place in it. Here I am, a ten year old girl, standing before the basin in the blue-tiled bathroom, in our house, 43 Central Street, in the suburb of Lower Houghton, in Johannesburg, a city in South Africa, a country at the tip of Africa, a continent on the earth, the earth a planet in the galaxy, the galaxy...then I sip water, gargle, spit and go to bed. I never ask my brothers if they think about this.

Cigar

Our liquor cabinet has a drawer. It is here Dad keeps round coasters, bottle openers and forgotten corks, as well as an unopened wooden box of cigars, a gift from a patient. One Saturday afternoon, our parents safely napping, Eric, Roy and I decide to steal a cigar and go smoke it on the bottom lawn, far from the house. We cut the red ribbon off the cigar box, lift the lid; an aroma of leather chairs and strong coffee waft up through the cellophane-wrapped cigars. Eric grabs one, I have matches and we race quietly for the bottom lawn, with Spotty and Kelly, our dogs, prancing around us. There we sit in a circle. Eric unwraps the cellophane and I throw the wrapping over our fence into the rough of the golf course. This disturbs a commotion of African ibises who flutter up cawing, then take their positions again on the willow tree branches.

"Rule number 1," says Roy, "Get rid of the evidence." Eric, the eldest at twelve, lights the cigar and takes a few puffs to get it going.

"Pass it!" I shout, then take a puff and pass it on to Roy.

"Terrific!" Roy says. We puff and pass it along.

"Best thing that's happened in all of my eight years," says Roy.

After my third draw I don't feel that great, and I see Eric and Roy slowing down too. We keep passing and puffing in silence.

Eric finally says, "I've had enough."

Roy says, "I feel sick."

"Me too," I reply. The cigar has hardly been smoked.

"I think I'm going to vomit," says Roy, tries to get up, falls back, curls up on the grass. Spotty rests his nose on Roy's knee, looks at Eric and me with mournful eyes. Eric stubs the cigar into the ground.

Roy moans. We all find a spot on the lawn and lie there. Phineas comes walking toward us pushing the wheelbarrow. He stops and looks at us, "Yinindaba?" he asks, "What goes on here?"

Eric lifts his head, "Phineas, do you want a cigar?"

"Sure!" he laughs, no questions asked as he puts the dead cigar into his overall pocket, keeps walking, leaving us to recover.

School

Spotty, our fox terrier, follows us to Houghton Primary School, and at that morning's assembly, as we all recite the Lord's Prayer, I look up and see him jumping on Mr. Gordon, our Principal, who is leading us. He tries to shake off the dog, without skipping a word or changing his rhythm. 'Who art in Heaven," He swats a long arm at the dog, which only excites Spotty further, "Hallowed be Thy name," He kicks at Spotty. The other teachers stand with their eyes closed, their heads bowed, but there are titters from among assembled pupils, who nudge their neighbors and point up to the platform. We listen to Mr. Gordon reciting "lead us not into temptation" and watch him kick at Spotty, who thinks this is a game and dances around Mr. Gordon's legs. At the end of prayers he thunders, "Does anybody know to whom this dog belongs?" My brothers and I are silent and Spotty does not give us away by sniffing us out, but rather suddenly, loses interest in Houghton Primary School and runs off.

Heaven is the closing bell. It is joined by the chimes of Pappacello's ice-cream seller. "Lollies, lollies," shouts the young, black ice cream vendor, outside the school gates. "Ma, Ma, buy us an ice-cream," respond hordes of escaping children. The vendor lifts the lid and a cloud of dry ice drifts up and hangs over the cart. When it clears, we can see rows of Eskimo Pies, rows of orange, red and green ice lollies, cups of vanilla, chocolate or strawberry, with small flat wooden spoons stuck to the lids. Business is brisk, ice-cream and money hurriedly change hands, and children, their grey socks now around their ankles, their ties askew, their blazers half hanging off them, wander off, carrying their treats.

A new ice-cream comes on the market in the early fifties and is first introduced to us outside the school gates. It is called sherbet and it is the best! Sherbet is served in cups of glorious flavors, peppermint, lemon and pineapple. No longer do we have to choose between the three previously offered ice-creams, chocolate, vanilla or strawberry. Occasionally, on an especially hot afternoon, a mother buys the African "ice cream boy," a grown man, a lollie and everyone smiles.

"Thank you Madam."

"You are welcome, Jim."

His name is not Jim, Black men are often called Jim by whites. The government kept changing the names of the entire black population. They are alternatively referred to as non-whites, non-Europeans, black, Bantu, African, natives – and those are only the polite names.

Sports Day is one of the highlights of the school year for me. Mom usually wins the Mother's race, her dark hair streams behind her as she and the other mothers race barefoot, their brightly patterned cotton skirts billowing around them. Their shrieks of laughter, make us all smile as we cheer them on from the grandstand.

We never ask Dad if he is going to run in the Father's race. He is far too staid and he is not a sportsman.

"He's a good man," my mother tells us, when he declines to join us in any sporting activity, "he just doesn't play sport, that's all."

One year Dougie and Kate Smollan's father, Fred, trips while running in the Father's race during sports day and the ground shakes. He is a Rugby Springbok and a huge man. He is so fit, that even after he picks himself up, he passes the other fathers, to win the race.

Our houses are Eland, Kudu, Impala and Sable. I am in Kudu House and wear my yellow rosette with pride, love screaming our war cry during races; "Boomalaka, boomalaka, Rah! Rah! RAH!, chickalaka, chickalaka, hah! Hah! HAH!, Who ya gonna yell for? Kudu Rah!! Sable has green rosettes, Impala, red rosettes and Eland, blue. We all lift our animal horns high after each event won. My mother tells me she recognizes me, from where they are sitting in the parent's grandstand. She points me out to Dad. "All we can see of you Tanya, are your tonsils, all day long!"

"Fight! Fight!" the word spreads around the playing field at break and children run to where a crowd gathers. Some of us are jumping rope, ignore the stampede, but when I hear, "It's your brother and Neil Ramsey," I race to where a circle has formed. Neil is known as the school bully. He has a criminal's face at 13, a broken nose, a mean thin mouth and lifeless eyes. There is always dried egg on his school sweater. He eventually is pushed up to Standard Five, the last year of Primary School. Roy is in Standard Two. Neil's socks rumple around his ankles and he circles Roy, with his fists in front of his swaying mean face. Roy's ready, and I join the crowd yelling "Hit him, hit him!" He was bigger but Roy's fitter and he gets in the first punch. "Go Roy!" we yell. Then Neil rushes, pounds him. Roy stumbles backward, Neil jumps on top of him. They both fall to the ground, dust rises. Legs and arms swing. Someone jumps in front of me and I can't see them anymore. Suddenly, a cry goes up, "Break it up!" The playground teacher pushes in, and pulls the two apart. I see Roy's nose is bleeding. The bell goes for the end of the break and the crowd walks back to the classrooms. Neil slinks off with two cronies. When their backs are turned, Roy's young friends rush up to him and pat him on the dusty back of his sweater. "Well done! You showed him." I walk up to Roy. He sees me and smiles,

"I gave it a go! Good fight hey?"

"Terrific!" I answer and throw my arms around him, help him dust the sand off his grey shorts and give him a tissue to wipe his nose.

Dad goes over my homework, especially when tests come up. The subject is the Great Trek of 1835, the organized exodus of 10,000 Boers, who left the Cape and traveled north in covered wagons, to get away from the British yoke and begin a new social order in South Africa governing themselves, with the blessing and guidance of God.

I am fascinated by an offshoot of trekkers who left the main party only to perish in the desert. This became known as the Dorsland Trek. Every question my Dad asks, I answer hurriedly, waiting for him to ask me about the Dorsland Trek.

"Tanya, why was the Great Trek so important?"

"Because it was the central event in the history of white men in South Africa." (a direct quote from our history book.)

"Do you understand what that means?"

"Yes Dad, it means whites expanded into areas previously unoccupied by other whites. But Dad ask me about the Dorsland Trek."

He ignores me.

"How did they defend themselves when natives attacked?"

"Ach man Dad, they formed a laager."

He looks at me, waiting for a fuller explanation.

"They placed the wagons in a circle, put thorn bushes in the gaps and between the spokes of the wheels. Then it was a battle between guns and flying assegais. (spears). Now can I tell you about the Dorsland trekkers?"

I know every detail, how everyone had eventually died of thirst, were buried under a Wag-n-bietjie (Wait-a-Bit) tree in the desert.

His patience runs out.

He says, "That was so unimportant, it did not change history at all. Forget about it! Give me three names of the leaders of the Great Trek."

"Potgieter, Celliers, Retief," I mumble.

"Good," he says closing my history book. He leaves me with my thoughts of those poor Dorsland trekkers. What they went through, and they didn't change history at all.

Budgies

I spend a lot of time in the aviary. I climb in through a raised door, hardly having to stoop at all. Then once in, walk upright twenty steps to the back, and thirty steps from one side to the other. Budgies and their breeding boxes are nailed along the back wall. Rabbits and guinea pigs share the sandy floor. There is a high, slanted tiled ceiling, similar to the one on the main house. Budgies sit on the cross bars, which run the length of the cage. When I walk in each day to feed them, there is a whirr of wings, as yellow, green, blue and multi-coloured small birds fly desperately around, coming to perch on the cross bars, while I empty the seed onto their tray, which is suspended five feet above the "rodents" as my Granny dismissively calls the guinea pigs and rabbits, on the one occasion she came to see the aviary.

Didi, my closest girlfriend, and I, had cleaned out the huge cage months before, carrying old empty coal bags, half filled cement bags, broken ladders, empty flower pots, until finally the space emptied. I buy the first budgies with pocket money. The first guinea pigs and rabbits are gifts.

After a few months I have far too many guinea pigs and rabbits and have to give them away at school but the budgies never breed. A friend tells me to feed them with widgem oil. It has Vitamin E in it, and that, she assures me will make them breed. So I ask Dad, - he should know – he is a gynecologist - to bring home some widgem oil, so the budgies will breed. He tells me he has never heard of it, but I have, so I nag him everyday to bring me some widgem oil.

"Tanya," he eventually says, "speak slowly. I think I know what you are asking for, it's called wheatgerm oil."

"Dad," I say in exasperation, "that's what I've been telling you all the time."

The next night he brings home a bottle. I rush down to the aviary, sprinkle some oil on the seeds. Everyday, until the bottle is empty, I sprinkle oil and after a few days, drag a ladder into the aviary and peep into the breeding boxes to see if anything is happening. Nothing does for the longest time. Then I start to find two or three eggs in a few boxes. I try not to look all the time, because the mother budgies don't like me looking in the boxes. I try to make sure they are feeding or flying when I look. Babies are born. They are the ugliest things I have ever seen. Their beaks are huge compared to their thin little heads and ugly grey feathers. But mainly they are pink and bald. Their mothers must think they are ugly too, because they throw them out of the breeding boxes onto the hard sand below. When I find babies still alive, I feed them with a nose dropper, but it never works. The poor little things all die. Some are so lifeless, it is hard to tell if they are already dead as I squeeze their beaks open and try to feed them.

Puppies

I have much more luck with Kelly's puppies when I am fourteen. Kelly is my wire haired terrier. Just before we break up for the long winter holidays, she has puppies. On the second morning, I rush down to the store room we have emptied for her. She is lying dead while the puppies suckle. I run upstairs crying, to tell the family what has happened. Mom asks Phineas to put Kelly and her five puppies, whose eyes are still closed, in a big cardboard box, and to put the box on the backseat of her car. She and I drive to the veterinarian. He examines Kelly, tells us she died of milk fever. He also said probably the puppies will die as there is no-one to feed them and they are so young. I say I will feed them. He looks down at me, "Young lady, it is a full time job, do you have the time?" So I tell him, we have just broken up for the winter holidays. I have five weeks, all day to feed the puppies.

He says, "Well, you can try."

He gives Mom the formula and we leave Kelly with him and take the puppies home. I feed them every two hours in the beginning with a baby's bottle. Mom and Evalina make up the formula at first, before they teach me how to do it. Feeding them does take all my time, but that's all I want to do anyway. By the time the fifth puppy is fed, it is time to start on the first one again. Days go by, their eyes open, they stumble around, fall over each other. Then weeks go by and I don't have to feed them so much. One day the veterinarian says to stop the bottle feeding. The puppies can now drink out of saucers. All the puppies live. We give them away to friends. The Smollans call theirs Elvis and we see him often. We keep two, although it takes days to persuade my father. He does not like dogs and calls all of them Voetsak! (It means scram in Afrikaans.)

146

Visiting Grandparents

"Noordhoek" my grandparent's home covers a full suburban block in Houghton. We love visiting, especially on Sundays after a Saturday horse race, when the talk is of how Grandpa's horses ran, and how Gran "had a flutter on the main race." Children are not allowed to go to the racetrack with the adults by law, but Grandpa often takes us to his stud farm in Vrede in the Orange Free State to see the horses and to be with his trainer Mr. Eatwell, an enormous man who lives up to his name. Mr. Eatwell's wife is a tiny woman. His side of the bed has a deep bowl, Eric tells me it is because a giant sleeps there- Mr. Eatwell.

We run around my grandparent's huge garden, among the stocks in winter, and up and down stairs and down the long corridor with bedrooms and bathrooms, the pink tiled, blue tiled and lemon colored tiled. Portraits of my uncle and aunts are displayed along the upstairs gallery wall. Mom's is of her in jodhpurs and a tee shirt; aunt Barbara's long hair hangs down in ringlets and aunt Valerie's party dress is classic 1930's. Uncle Jerry's is a schoolboy in King Edward VII School uniform.

Aunt Valerie contracted meningitis and polio and became crippled when she was thirteen. My Grandparents took her all over the world to try and get her cured – all to no avail. When they returned home, they built an indoor swimming pool for her, as one of the doctors suggested her muscles would respond to swimming exercises. I clearly remember the day she died, she was thirty years old. Her friend Jerry Milne walked down the staircase sobbing into a lace handkerchief.

Sunday morning tea, when Granny's two sisters arrive with their families is a fun time. They call each other by their Russian names, Fraide, Zlat and Hinde (names never heard when they are in company… then they use their English names, Freda, Zena and Ida.) The family emigrated from Suvalki a small town on the Polish-Russian border. They and their brother Ben, went first to Leeds in Yorkshire, and then ultimately my great grandfather decided to bring his family to South Africa.

The sisters are close and have shared many memories, they have a shorthand language. One of the favorite stories is a remembered seaside conversation, held on Muizenberg beach, near Cape Town. The group is sitting on deck chairs on the beach, the men in their grey flannels, the women in knitted swimsuits. Uncle Bernard, then a young boy, comes running over shouting the news, "Hitler's dead! Hitler's dead!" Granny's mother, only known to me as a photograph of an elderly lady with a grey bun, says,

"Oh, that's too terrible!"

The family group look at her stunned,

"Mother, Hitler's dead!"

"Who?"

"Hitler!" they all shout.

"Oh, I thought Bernard said Krickler," she responds, referring to the gentleman who owns the boarding house where she stays for the vacation.

The sisters remember meeting an acquaintance on the beach at Muizenberg. They go through the same conversation which is repeated by different groups along the entire beach, "When did you arrive?" "How long are you staying?" "How's your holiday, so far?" "When are you going back?"

"We are enjoying ourselves, we only arrived yesterday but we are going back tomorrow."

"You are going back tomorrow!?" "Why so soon?"

"Haven't you heard?"

"Heard what?"

"Hitler's army is in Retreat."

They fall about laughing, almost spilling their tea and explain to the listening children Retreat is the next town down the railway line to the vacation spot.

Grandpa shakes his head, "Marvelous!" He says sarcastically, "She always was a bloody fool."

"And her husband was no better." adds Zlat aka Auntie Zena.

Then the three sisters, who have been taught by their mother to be snobs, really get into it, and Russian or Yiddish expressions fly around the verandah, "Eh, a kuchie fykie, if there ever was one."

"You're right Hindele, a grobbie dundie!"

"A pas goodnik, and no oil painting either!" Fraide has the last word.

I don't understand what they are saying but it is not complimentary.

It is always great fun in Granny Freda's company. She is very generous to her extended family, has a great sense of humor and a positive way of looking at the world. She was the first woman to own a car in Johannesburg.

I love her expressions. We are at a restaurant one night, she spies a very short man, and she says with a twinkle in her eye, "He can take a walk under the table."

I ask Dad about his family background, because I understand our history did not begin in South Africa, but only ever get vague answers. Maybe it is because his mother died when he was very young in the flu pandemic of 1918, and he did not get a chance to ask her. His father died many years before we were born. His family is more interested in the present and the future than their past.

He does tell me they were very poor and when he won a medical scholarship to Edinburgh University he traveled in the ship with a convict as a room mate. The convict was shackled to the bed.

"Ooh Dad, why did you travel like that?" I ask.

"Because," he answers, "there was no cheaper fare."

Mealtimes are awaited celebrations at our grandparents, be it eleven or four o clock tea on the deep verandah, with elegant women and talkative men eating scones, or Granny's chocolate cake, which is about five inches high, covered with chocolate icing, and then red or emerald green cherries, as well as chocolate vermicelli. Sometimes it is casual meals in the breakfast room, and very occasionally more formal meals in the dining room. The living room is enormous, a huge fireplace at the far end, groups of sofas and chairs fill the rest of the room. Windows overlook the garden. Grandpa's study with its comfortable brown leather sofa and two huge brown leather chairs is cozy and perfect for losing oneself in one of the books taken from his library which take the place of walls in that room. There are many people living in the back yard, three gardeners, maids and a cook. Wilson, the chef, calls himself "oldie man" from the time I first remember meeting him in the fifties. He is a gentle Zimbabwean and he will be with my Grandmother, long after aunt Valerie dies, long after Noordhoek is sold, after Grandpa dies. Wilson and Granny move into their old age together. They still both dress for dinner, she in her cashmere skirts and cardigans, complete with her necklace of pearls, he in his waiter's white suit, white gloves and red sash. Wilson always sets the table, as he has done since the 1950's when he first worked for the family. There is only one place setting now, but still with crystal glass, monogrammed cutlery, linen napkin He stands, after serving her, as he always has done, in the corner of the dining room. Usually it is a three course meal. Her favorite, hot tomato soup and melba toast followed by an entrée with vegetables and very often a dessert of fruit salad.

I speak to him in the kitchen in the mid 1970's. He tells me, "Oldie man is too sick now."

I ask what is bothering him.

"Oh," he sighs, "my eyes, my heart, I want to go home and sit now."

His home in Rhodesia (Zimbabwe) is where his wife waits on their small plot of land, with his children whom he has hardly seen and who now have children of their own.

"You should go Wilson, you have been away so long."

"Oh," he sighs again, "But who will watch Granny?"

He stays until Granny passes away in 1978. After a few days of helping us pack up her place, Wilson allows himself to retire and go back home, where we write letters and keep in touch until his death.

One day Mom's driving the lift club (car pool) home after school and we are passed by a fire engine, siren wailing. "Follow him Ma!" and she does, right up the driveway of my grandparents house. Afterwards when the fire is out, and the firemen have gone, Eric runs outside, where we are all still standing, looking up at the charred gable. He holds a black jacket with brass buttons, "one of the firemen has forgotten his jacket." My elegant Grandmother, who resembles Marlene Dietrich, takes one look and retrieves her haute couture French jacket, "That is mine, thank you very much, I will have it now."

Gran used to bake every Friday and it was our custom to visit her on Saturday mornings. We would run immediately to the pantry, where biscuits were arranged on trays like jewels. There were square ones with chocolate icing and red cherries, round ones with vanilla icing and green cherries, almond tartlets, scones, nut balls, cocoa meringues. Swiss rolls with raspberry jam. Also in the pantry sat Zotwe, an old sourpuss employee of my grandparents, who only ever seemed to wear slippers with a pom-pom of colored wool on the top. "Granny says, wait until teatime!" She would fix us with her thin eyes.

"AGH, puleeze Zottie, only one." we would moan.

"No, get out of my pantry!" and she would half stand as if to chase us.

We are made to feel much more welcome by Esther, Evalina and Phineas and it is a treat to eat with them. We sit in a circle in the backyard, Esther's legs straight out in front of her, her shoes kicked off and her doek which she wears low on her forehead and tied behind her neck is undone, her springy hair free and wild. Phineas sits on an upturned wooden box. I am cradled in Evalina's arms on a low beach chair. They have discarded the pantomime of their roles in my parents' house and are three grown-ups enjoying a meal. We share putu, the stiff mealie meal which tastes of smoke and gravy. Evie teaches me how to sweep the putu across the plate, gather gravy, then stuff it into your mouth and suck off your fingers. She always says, "It is nutritious and delicious!" Other days we chew on the gristle of "boy's meat," which my mother buys at the butchers, in the glass case, separate from Whites cuts of meat. We drink hot, sweet tea from tin mugs to wash down the huge slabs of brown bread lathered in peanut butter. Drinking this way feels very daring as most white children are told never to drink from the same cup as the servants. The stories told are illustrated with body movements, many exclamations of "Aikona! No! and retorts of "Struze God." And "Yo,yo,yo!" and when thanked for the meal, they smile and say, "Hazeku ndaba," No problem. These feasts with the hearty laughter and the feeling of goodwill are so much more enjoyable than watching our table manners in the dining room, with its linen tablecloth and silver cutlery, and "finish your food, children are starving in Europe."

Adult Dinner Parties

We are fed in the kitchen on the nights our parent's give dinner parties for my Dad's colleagues. After our supper I like to stay hidden in the dark, halfway up the stairs when the doorbell rings, so I can see the guests arrive. The wives, to a woman, wear fox wraps, summer or winter, their beady eyes, both the fox and the women, glinting in the hallway lamp. In they come, neurologists, general practitioners, orthopedic surgeons, serious bespectacled gentlemen and their quiet unobtrusive wives, all shepherded into the lounge. The conversation never rises above a murmur. The next morning my mother looks fatigued. I don't know how she stands it.

Play Date

Sometimes Mom arranges for me to play with Emily Schub, who lives up the road. Her Dad is a surgeon, a colleague of my Dad's. He's married to a tiny mouse of a woman. Granny says she can take a walk under a table.

Their somber house smells both musty and antiseptic. Added to the smell, it is a dark house, an aberration in Africa. The walls are mahogany wood, the furniture is heavy European teak, the maroon velvet drapes, even though tied back, almost cover the tiny windows. Lamps are lit at noon.

Emily and I, both nine years old play quiet games. Around four o' clock a timid maid carries in a tray, on which are two glasses of pale Oros, a drop of orangeade and the rest water, and two lemon cream biscuits. The servants work quietly. The entire house is hushed. I am used to our jovial cook Esther and Evelina, our nanny, cackling with laughter as they shout stories to each other, or tease Phineas, the gardener, when he comes to our kitchen door with the mail.

When the afternoon ends, I whisper, "Goodbye, Mrs. Schub." She sits busy with embroidery while she listens to "Women's World," on the radio.

"Thank you for having me."

The little dog at her feet opens one eye to look at me, sighs, curls tighter into himself. I click the garden gate gently, then tear down Central Street on my bike, shouting out verses of Elvis' "Ya ain't a nothin' but a hound dog" or "I'm proud to say, I'm inna love YEAH! All shook up!" as loud as I can, re-introducing life-saving noise into my world. My dogs hear me coming and are frantic with an excitement which I encourage and escalate as we whoop

154

around the lawn, physically expelling the cobwebby decorum of the Schub's home. A few days later Dad tells us he been to attend to one of the sisters at the Carmelite Nunnery – the order of nuns who have taken a vow of silence. I tell him they must have done their training at the Schubs.

Rusty Coates

Red-haired Rusty Coates stays with us for a week. His father is a Pan Am pilot, a friend of Uncle Jerry. He and 16 year old Rusty are visiting from America. My mother tells us at breakfast one morning, that the Russians have sent Sputnik, a spacecraft into space. Eric, Roy and I are very impressed, but Rusty, a few years older than us, slowly puts his knife and fork down, looks at my mother and says, "Do you really believe that?"

The next morning when our family enthusiastically confirms we spotted the blip crossing the heavens during the night, he keeps eating his breakfast.

He thinks everyone in South Africa is mad anyway. During the first few days he's with us, we drive into the city of Johannesburg to show him around. We take him to the Johannesburg Zoo. He walks ahead of everyone, goes through the entrance marked non-European. South African public life, be it transport, public places or facilities, such as toilets and benches have signs painted on them - European (meaning white) and non-European (meaning non-white). Segregation is strictly enforced.

Immediately a white guard approaches Rusty, shouts,

"Hey! You! You are not allowed through this entrance. It is for non-Europeans."

The following conversation takes place.

"Well I am a non-European."

"No! You are not!"

"Yes. I am."

"You are a white man."

"I know I'm a white man."

"Then you must go through the European entrance!"

"But I'm not a European. I am American."

"What!!?"

At this point my mother arrives, tries to explain the South African way of life to Rusty. Like the guard, she gets nowhere with him. Finally she says, "Rusty, just walk where you see us walking."

"Jeez Louise," is all he says.

Piano Lessons

Every Tuesday afternoon for five years the doorbell rings at four 'o clock and Mrs Sheftz, the piano teacher, overweight and harried, stands there panting. She hurries in to the lounge, carrying a black briefcase with worn leather straps and an oversized handbag. She slaps some music sheets in front of me. "Play these scales," she says letting out a deep sigh and kicking off her shoes. She sits next to me and I follow her fingers as they move along the page. Soon her fingers slip and I sneak a sideways glance at her. Her mouth is open and her head has fallen to one side. When it happens the first time, I play on without her guidance as I know the scales. We never play anything but scales.

However week after week, when this happens I play whatever notes my fingers hit as I look at her toes peeping through torn stockings. I sometimes play "thunder", the low notes, loudly, and she stirs, runs her fingers along the lines of the music sheet. My most fun is if Spotty, my fox terrier is in the room. If he is, after making sure Mrs. Sheftz is dozing, I play the "Lightening" notes, the high ones, until Spotty responds by lifting his head and yowling in tune to the notes. I imitate my dog, pretending we are a duo, straining my neck and imitating him soundlessly. This part of our act wakens Mrs.Sheftz, who looks at me in a startled way, brings Evalina to the door, and banishes Spotty from the room. I don't want to learn the piano and she is too tired to teach, so our arrangement suits both of us. I spend the half hour playing, hitting sequences of notes and pumping the pedal as if I am a maestro in a packed concert hall, waving to appreciative audiences and nodding my head to left and right to acknowledge applause. I also watch her as I can't imagine someone sleeping sitting up, without a backrest. She never falls over. I always end these concerts with my signature tune, "Mister Whatchyoucallit what you doin tonight, Hope you're in the mood, cos I'm feeling just right!" over and over until she breathes in deeply, a snore wakes her, she blinks her eyes and comes out of her coma. "Quite good child, you are coming along nicely." Then she pushes her swollen feet into her old bent, cracked black shoes, gathers up her oversize handbag and I see her to the door.

Infatuation

Most days, after four o' clock afternoon tea, I run up and down the top lawn, holding a field-hockey stick and dribbling a ball. I am waiting for Harrow Brenner, our blonde eighteen year old next door neighbor, who is at University and drives a white Saab. He is German. I have read and cried over "The Diary of Anne Frank" and I think in some way, which I don't understand, I want this German man to fall in love with me, a fourteen year old Jewish girl. His father might have been a Nazi, I think, but he is too young. Anyway the war is over and we are living a prosperous life in South Africa. Even though our daily lives are secure, we know everything is not great here either. The Nationalists are in power and probably if it wasn't for the blacks, "the swart gevaar", (the black danger) as they are called, the government would be more openly anti-Semitic. They regard most Jews as Communists and they hate Communists. The way they see it, if you are not Afrikaans, you are an outsider, an interloper in their country. Our lives are so good. As whites and as Jews, we have nothing to fear from them and we regard the Nationalist Government with disdain. My parents are not overly political. They vote for the Opposition Party and Mom canvasses for Helen Suzman for Parliament, when she is the lone Member for Houghton.

My hockey game improves, dribbling the ball between obstacles I place on the lawn, but the main obstacle is I am only fourteen and Harrow's eighteen. Occasionally I time it right and am racing toward his fence, swerving the ball around the stones I have placed in a line down the lawn. He waves and we talk over the fence, behind the tall purple and magenta foxgloves, but sometimes his car turns into the driveway and I am with my back turned at the far end of the lawn. He drives directly into their garage and walks indoors. Field hockey practice goes on for months. One day I walk into our kitchen and there on the table is a gift for me.

"Who brought this?" I ask Esther, I am desperate to know every detail.

"A delivery man," she replies, more interested in basting that evening's chicken. My birthday is the next day. The card, which I keep in my desk for months, until the ink is smudged and the corners worn, says, "Happy Birthday to a lovely girl, Fondly, Harrow." At that moment I have never been happier. Along with the card is a gift, my first bottle of perfume, L'Heure Bleu by Guerlain. That night I dab it on sparingly behind each ear, as I have seen Mom do, and go down to dinner, where my brothers sniff and ask,

"Phew, what's that smell?"

I look at Mom and exchange a look that says, "Savages, what do they know?" and I reply, "It is called perfume. A man gave it to me."

Tennis

Tennis is my racket and I play in the first team at Houghton Government Primary school, even though I am too short to see over the net. No problem, I see through it. Phineas and I paint a line against a wall of our house, the height of a net, and I practice driving the ball, just above the line. I spend hours doing this. The dining-room window, way above the line, is in the middle of the right hand service box. Occasionally, I slam the ball wild, and watch with horror as the ball careens toward the window, glass shatters. "Hau!" I hear, as fierce Esther, barrels through the garage door. "Stop this bloody tennis!" That night at dinner, my father wipes his mouth with the linen napkin, says, "Tanya, I believe you broke the window again." He shakes his head, turns to cut his steak. My Mom asks Phineas, who has now changed from his gardener's overalls into a white waiter's suit to brick up the window. Phineas gives me a small nod. After that everyone is much calmer.

My Grandfather sometimes hits a ball to me, after his men's Sunday morning tennis. He is the one who teaches me how to hit it low and hard down the tram-lines. He plays in long white linen trousers and a long-sleeved shirt. He tells me the story of twins, whose father is a regular player on my Grandparents' court. Most of the tennis group are first generation South Africans having emigrated from Eastern Europe. The twins play polo and the joke is, "From Poland to polo in one chukka."

Later in high school, when I am a boarder at a school in Johannesburg, Mom is one of the mothers who volunteer to drive the tennis team to our away games. She treats us to Coca-Cola and cake, in cafes, before driving us back to school. One day,

162

a match at Ellis Park ends and four of us pile into Mom's little black Austen and drive back to school as the heaven's open and a torrential rainstorm begins. People say you can set your watch by the 5:00 p.m. highveld summer storms. Halfway up Nugget Hill, the steepest hill in the city, our car begins sliding backwards. Mom guns it up two or three times, all of us leaning forward as if to help it gain the top of the hill, but each time, the road is too slippery and water running down the hill, prevents us from reaching the top. Finally at the bottom of the hill, Mom turns the car around and reverses easily up, with the girls in the back seat shouting directions until finally we crest in Berea. We have other adventures in Mom's car. During strikes by blacks when their bus or taxi fare is raised, thousands of them stage a "walk-to-work" campaign, boycotting the buses and taxis. White housewives drive along the main routes into the city and give rides to the blacks, for as long as the boycott lasts.

Bicycles

Bicycles are a big deal. Twelve year old Koos Van de Merwe, Dr. van der Merwe's son, uses his to ride every day after school to the corner of 11th Avenue and Central Street, where he waits for accidents to happen. He then comes back to report to us what he has seen. "Hell man, you should have seen, this Packard was pranged hey." He could not have been the only one watching as one day he dejectedly tells us, traffic lights had been installed on that corner and his fun was over.

Our gang rides all around the neighborhood, often carrying tennis rackets or swim suits, stopping off for a swim or a game and then riding to the next house. Peter Simpson's backside can hardly fit on the saddle. Andrew Sacks and Colin Goldberg, the two ducktails of the crowd, put playing cards in the spokes of the wheels, and imagine as they peddle they are on Harley Davidsons. The cards revolve, snap like an engine against the spokes. Our greatest fun is to go riding after a summer storm has thrown lavender jacaranda blossoms onto the pavement. They pop with a resounding snap and it feels powerful and exciting, like Guy Fawkes firecrackers on a summer's afternoon. We keep our bikes in the shed which smells like a florist as crushed blossoms cling to the wheels. Days later as we ride, the perfumed air rises as the wheels rotate. Our bike tours around the neighborhood break up when Rodney Morgan comes with a chopper and chops up Eric's bike. Rodney's parents and our parents sort out the problem but they forbid us to play with those children, ever again.

1960's
Saturday Matinee

During school holidays on Saturday afternoons, Win, a close friend and I, dress in hoop skirts, under which we wear stiff netted petticoats, our waists cinched with wide belts and gypsy blouses, ride the "Europeans Only" red double-decker bus into town. The conductor, with his books of different colored cardboard tickets flicks his thumb down the change distributor which crosses his chest on a leather strap, and gives us back tickeys or sixpences in change. Our destination varies between The Colosseum, His Majesty's Theater, and The Empire, all in downtown Johannesburg. En route in our half-empty bus, we pass lines of Blacks at their stops waiting for the green, government-owned PUTCO buses, "Green Mambas" as they are called. Once in the city, we pass the department stores of Anstey's, Stuttafords, Greaterman's and John Orr's, with well dressed mannequins in their windows. Win and I sing the "Liftgirls lament," (the girls who operate the elevators in the department stores) a song made popular by Jeremy Taylor, an English folksinger, who sings at the Cul de Sac coffee bar. We know all the words and recite what can be bought on the different floors.

We watch the crowds from our upstairs front row seats, there are many more blacks than whites. We lurch down Jeppe Street where most of the doctors, including my father and uncles have their rooms. We pass our dentist, Dr. Stuppel's rooms. He always talks when the slow, loud drill is in your mouth and you can't answer because you are in such pain, plus the cotton wads, jammed between your gums and teeth, there to sop up the blood, make it impossible to say anything other than, "mmmmm".

When our stop comes we pull the cord, go down the bus stairs, past the sign which reads, DO NOT SPIT/MOENIE SPOEG NIE and out into the busy city streets, sixteen years old, free to enjoy lunch and a film. Young blacks dance and play penny whistles, while white men in suits and ties steer ladies in hats, hurriedly by. The whites look serious, while blacks sit in the gutters, their restaurants, in mid-town Johannesburg. They open loaves of bread, from which they pull out the insides, ball them up and push them into their mouths. They talk and laugh as traffic scoots by.

A uniformed usherette shows you to your seat, leading the way in the pitch dark with a flashlight. When your eyes get used to the light you see the world is a magical place of plush elegance, with cherubs painted on the walls and in one theatre, a starlit sky. On the bus home in the blinding light of day, we cry after seeing "Lili." For days after, we sing, "A song of love is a sad song…"

People dress for the Saturday night movies. Men in ties and jackets, buy their dates boxes of Black Magic chocolates. The audience is quiet during the South African National Anthem and later the British National Anthem. Popular British war movies are usually a family affair. We discuss The Dam Busters in the car driving home, and how the bomb had to drop just so, so it would bounce along the water and hit the dam wall and flood the Ruhr valley. Another tune that stays with us for months is from "Bridge on the River Kwai." My brothers and I and other friends all see that film; we agree Brits make the best war movies.

It is at the movies we first see Elvis the Pelvis gyrating to hisses from the older audience, "Disgusting!" "How awful!" "He should be banned!"

They would have enjoyed seeing Dame Margot Fonteyn dance Swan Lake one night, on a platform especially built into the side of the Zoo Lake. During the performance some of the resident swans swam nearby and seemed to be part of the corps de ballet.

The country does not have T.V. so radio and gramophones are our entertainment. When Trini Lopez came to Johannesburg, L.M. radio played La Bamba all day. And then of course there are parties on Saturday nights.

Saturday Nights

The party's at our house. Boys in long grey flannels and jackets stand against the wall sneaking awkward peeks at the girls across the room. The girls tug their skirts, ask each other, "Do I look O.K.?" and "Really? Did he really say he likes me?"

Elvis' "You ain't a nothin' but a hound dog" fills the room and a team of boys walk across, pull girls back to the center, until everyone is jiving. Roy is in charge of changing the 78's. His best friend Edwin helps. It's their job to keep the music going. Adults have been banned. The door to the garden is open and some boys walk outside to light up a cigarette or "rook" as they prefer to say, and also slug beer they have hidden from parents. Phineas and Esther carry in trays of hotdogs. The boys greet Phineas with cool confidence, "Howzit, chief!" He smiles, bears his dignity well, remains unreachable to them. It is a good party, later someone turns off the light, Elvis is exchanged for Pat Boone singing "Love Letters in the Sand," couples pull close. Later, we all sway to Ray Conniff. Edwin leaves to meet his parents. Roy goes to bed, as he doesn't like it when couples begin smooching. Lots of us are going steady and dance only with our boyfriends. At breakfast the next day Mom tells us a story. A gang of gate-crashers, ducktails in leather jackets, tight stovepipe jeans and brylcreamed hair arrive at the front door, on the other side of the house from where we are having our party. They stand on the marble terrace, one leans on the doorbell. My mother fills a bucket of cold water, carries it to an upstairs window above the front door, and empties it down on the gate crashers. The water hits the marble like a gun shot. The young thugs take off never to return.

Holidays

We didn't have to ask where we were going for the summer holidays. Driving the thousand miles to Cape Town was an annual event. I remember the "full house" breakfasts at the small Karoo hotels where we always broke the journey stopping overnight. The next morning, traveling through the Hex River Valley in the Cape, arriving eventually in the seaside resort of Muizenberg, with the warm waves of the Indian Ocean and miles of flour soft sand. Everyday, barefoot Malay fruit sellers with their pants rolled up, wearing hats with huge brims, walked down the beach, balancing laden baskets of fruit at either end of a pole slung across their shoulders, shouting, "Fresh fruit, lichees, mangoes, peachies, sweet as your mother's heart!" In the afternoons our mothers would wait for the fish sellers cart, heralded by a horn, which the driver blew to attract customers. He too would shout, "Get your fresh snoek, kabeljou, kingklip, any fresher, they would be swimming!" We would walk on the slopes of Table Mountain with my Uncle who taught us to sing, "I love to go awandering along a mountain path"… the boys were the chorus, who sang "Valderee, valderah, my knapsack on my back."

Once we drove to Lourenco Marques for a holiday, I thought the gates of the Polana Hotel, were the gates of the city.

Three days of the winter school holidays were usually spent in the Kruger National Park. We stayed at Skukuza camp, went out on early morning game drives and again in the late afternoons. We never tired of looking for game. My favorite was lion. The world is never the same after you have heard the full throated glory of a lion roar, even the series of grunts following is impressive and otherworldly. I remember a kill, with lionesses clawing, growling

169

and spitting over their prey, and then slinking away as the lion approached, regally and slowly lowered himself onto his haunches, began his meal as the females waited in the background.

My Grandparents took more sophisticated holidays. I remember our family group waving to my elegant Grandmother, dressed to the nines, as she paused at the entrance to a jet (after having climbed the five or six steps to the plane's door,) and her waving back to Africa, an all encompassing royal wave, before ducking her head and disappearing into the airplane. Sunday entertainment for many families was standing behind the picket fence at Parmietfontein Airport and watching planes take off and land.

Dr. Verwoerd–Prime Minister

I open the front door to Donny Gordon who my father is expecting for a meeting. They go into the lounge, Dad closes the door but not before saying, "We do not want to be disturbed," but I had to disturb them when Noonoo, my friend from school, telephoned to say, "Had I heard, Dr. Verwoerd had been shot at the Rand Easter Show. A man called David Pratt." The next morning's paper showed a picture of the Prime Minister, with blood pouring down his face. He lived. A few years later Tsafendas, a parliamentary messenger, stabbed Dr. Verwoerd and this time, "the architect of apartheid", as The Rand Daily Mail wrote, was dead.

1970's
Passbook

"The man is dead."

Five middle-aged black men stand in the warm South African night air outside our kitchen door, hats in hands, with the sad news that Simon Kopaopa has died. The person who speaks hands me a crinkled brown paper bag. Our maid has left for the day. I am alone in the house with the baby. Startled to see five strangers in our backyard (where is our watchdog?) I do not invite them in.

When they have gone and I have locked and bolted the door and am sipping my now lukewarm tea, I feel ashamed. They walked and took buses from who knows where to give us the news of the death of our gardener, and I did not invite them in, nor did I offer them anything to eat or drink.

I look through the paper bag. Simon's passbook is there with the overalls he was wearing the day he took ill. The overalls are washed, ironed and folded.

I show the passbook to my husband on his return and together we hatch a plan.

We have recently seen Athol Fugard's play about pass laws, "Sizwe Banzi is Dead." In apartheid South Africa, blacks are required to carry a passbook showing name, address and tribe, as well as white bureaucrat's decisions about where they may live and work. In the play someone who does not have a pass acquires a dead man's pass, assumes his identity and is now legal. My husband and I reckon, if it works in a play, it might work in real life.

The next morning we speak to Victor Ncube, a black Zimbabwean, who works for us, who lost his passbook and does not want to go to the authorities, as he fears he will be "endorsed out," back to Zimbabwe, where there is no work for him and never be allowed into South Africa again.

Every time there is a police raid, anxiety is high. He hides in our house. There would be all sorts of hell to pay if he is found, both for him and for us. We could go to court or get heavily fined for "harboring a potential terrorist" or whatever other accusation the police trump up. Victor likes the idea.

"That is an easy thing for me. I can change the picture, take Simon's out, put mine in." He smiles, "I will be Simon. I will be legal, hee hee!"

And so he becomes legal and never has pass trouble again.

JAPHET JHANJE VISITING US IN NEW YORK CITY
LEFT TO RIGHT CLAUDIE, JAPHET, TANYA, MIKE,
LENNY

Zimbabwean Reunion

"There is my father's kraal!" shouted Aaron Jhanje, from the front seat of the truck. We had met Aaron in the city of Harare and he was our guide to his father, Japhet's farm. We looked over the savannah toward a mountain where round thatch huts perched halfway up the slope.

The tall grass swished against the truck, sounding like it was sailing over the veldt. Our twenty year old daughter, Claudia, and I, were in the open back of the truck, sitting high on a four-inch foam mattress, buttressed by sacks of vegetables and fruit we had brought as gifts. Our eighteen year old son, Lenny, was not with us on this trip. He had gone to a friend's farm and we missed him.

Japhet, an illiterate Shona tribesman, had been my husband's family cook for forty-five years in South Africa. Now our family was visiting him for the first time on his farm in Zimbabwe. His children and grandchildren had written to us declaring June 21st, the day of our visit, National Hochschild/Jhanje Day. Everybody had taken the day off from school, housework, and farm work.

"Come in the dry season," Aaron had written months before when the reunion was being planned. He knew many farm roads wash away once the rains come.

Japhet is an integral part of the Hochschild family. When Len, Mike's father, died, Hazel, Mike's mother sat at the dining room table which was covered with bills, her head in her arms, quietly weeping. She felt a hand on her shoulder, heard Japhet saying, "Don't worry Madam, we will be all right."

As Aaron, Hazel's father, prepared for months to die, Japhet tenderly nursed him, bathed, fed, dressed and sat with him in the garden.

Japhet's heroic story will never be known, since he is such a reticent man. After one vacation back to Zimbabwe, Japhet lost his papers to reenter South Africa. He crossed the crocodile infested Limpopo River, walked through lion country, tied himself to trees at night with his belt, until he finally arrived at the Hochschild front door in the suburb of Johannesburg. Hazel remembers, "He was like a specter."

Once he had convalesced, sitting in the garden in the sun, and being fed, Hazel asked him why he had done it. He simply replied,

"I owed the Baas $60."

Many people taught Japhet his culinary repertoire. They included grandmothers, friends of the family and especially Francisco, an Italian prisoner-of war, brought to the house on weekends, by Uncle Bill, the Commandant of the camp. Whenever given a recipe, he would find Simon, the gardener, who would read it to him. Japhet was illiterate It would be in Japhet's memory for ever.

He cooked to please and he cooked with pleasure. His party pea soup, mint green, his cannelloni, redolent of Tuscany, his mille feuille floated. A person would kill for one bite of his bread, hot from the oven, his beef Wellington was a party favorite.

The Hochschild sons left for boarding school with the taste of Japhet's ox tail stew on their tongues, and returned to find their favorite ravioli or steak and kidney pie, followed by home made ice-cream and the stickiest toffee sauce.

Japhet's chocolate éclairs glistened, his Cornish hens, chicken pies, duck a la Japh became family favorites.

His daily diet was nyama (meat) and sudsa (polenta), with a rich brown gravy. Huge tin mugs of steaming black tea, to which milk and two or three teaspoons of sugar was added, accompanied the meal.

After Mike and I married, Japhet taught me to cook. I use his standards as my own. He is a constant presence in my kitchen.

"We are nearly there!"

Aaron pointed to a right turn past some harvested cotton-fields. A group of people ran toward the dust-storm our truck had kicked up. Toddlers wearing multicolored beaded necklaces and belts ran after barefoot boys and girls in shorts and T shirts. Two curs, looking more like coyotes than dogs, barked with excitement. The colorful sarongs of the women flapped across their ankles. Three older boys wore grey flannel school pants and white shirts.

As we slowed to a stop, the children surged forward to crowd around the vehicle, banging on the hood. They laughed and shouted, "Welcome! Welcome Hochschilds!"

"I am Edmond," a teenage boy said grinning as he stuck his hand into my husband Mike's, across the open window.

"Edmond! I am Claudia," our daughter shouted from the back of the truck to her pen-pal she had never met.

"Ah, you are Claudie, I can see from the photo you sent me." He jumped up onto the back of the truck and grasped Claudie's hand.

Informal introductions were made after we had all stepped out of the truck. The curs crept around our ankles growling, showing yellow fangs. One of the elder boys chased them away,

We walked to a hut where Japhet, now an elderly man, was waiting for us. Shy and formal, he greeted us by shaking hands. We wanted to throw our arms around him.

"Do you still magic up your souffles, and your chocolate mousses Japh?" asked Hazel, who by her own admission can't boil an egg.

"No," he answered, looking at his wife standing behind him, "Tilda cooks for me at home."

He led us to the boma, a large open room. A sofa, wooden chairs and reed mats were arranged in a huge circle. He invited us to sit down.

Hazel was seated next to Japhet on the sofa. Tilda was on his other side. He was wearing his best suit and a tie. Mike was next to his mother, I was next to Mike. Claudie was on a reed mat, cradling a baby. Japhet's sister, sat on a mat with children surrounding her. Mabel, the oldest daughter sat on a wooden chair, her sons, Darron. Rodwell, Edmond and Lloyd sat behind her. Everyone else took their places on reed mats.

Aaron stood up,

"My father and his family welcome you to our farm. We begin our day with prayer, then the women sing a song of welcome."

We bowed our heads. I peeked at Mike, saw him wipe a tear from his eyes. He was with the elders of our two tribes. The prayer was in Shona, when it was completed all the women lifted their heads and sang two verses of a song. We could not understand the words but felt the meaning. The sound of their clear tones washed over us and up into the hills.

Two young women came in carrying a huge basin filled with water, and placed it on the trestle table.

"Please wash your hands," smiled Japhet, "We will have tea."

Hazel looked at the basin,

"Japh, you STILL have the basin. Remember we used to bathe the boys in it forty-five years ago!"

They laughed.

Japhet's daughter Lucia had baked cupcakes.

Flies settled on the cupcakes and the rims of the teacups, the only irritant to this excellent tea party. Everyone studiously ignored them.

After tea, sixteen of us piled into the truck. Mike, Hazel and Japhet sat in the front. We drove to the high school to meet the headmaster. He and Japhet, are the two most important men in the district. Japhet is the school treasurer.

Introductions were made; teachers and groups of students stood and stared at us. We were dressed differently, we did not know their language, we were strangers. Children suppressed giggles behind their hands. The headmaster took us on a tour of the school.

There are eight teachers for five hundred students. The library needs more books. Posters in the hallways explained the scourge of Aids.

Back at the kraal lunch had been prepared. Chickens grilled over an open wood fire in the kitchen hut. Loaves of hot bread, baked in a box, which had been set in the hot ashes, were cooling on racks. We were invited in. It was spotless. There was a hearth in the middle of a hard baked mud floor. Wooden shelves held pots, and pans. Plates were neatly stacked, and the basin of hot water was once again offered so we could wash our hands.

My mother-in-law whispered she needed to use the bathroom. I asked a young woman where it was, and she led us to a newly erected enclosed hut the size of a telephone booth, with "Eve" freshly painted on the door. An older hut stood some distance away. It had a freshly painted sign too, which read "Adam."

They had prepared the privies especially for us, and we were so grateful for their thoughtfulness. There was toilet paper on a nail on the door. It was dark inside. The rural johns in Africa are known as the long drop.

The same young woman showed us her sleeping hut, and told us huts are considered separate rooms within the kraal. The sleeping mats were rolled up on the floor, which was a mixture of earth compressed with cow dung and polished to a glossy smoothness. She also showed us a special area where she believed the ancestral spirits dwell.

Back in the boma the table had been set with a crocheted cloth. The women had made salads, wooden boxes filled with glass bottles of Coca-Cola, Ginger Beer and Orangeade stood in the center of the long trestle table. Once again we took up our places on various chairs and mats.

The children had lost their shyness and were regaling us with stories of farm life and pointing out landmarks. One little boy with liquid brown eyes announced next year National Hochschild/

Zhanje Day would be on a Tuesday. The boma erupted with happy laughter.

Aaron stood up again,

"Now we will introduce everyone to you."

He then went around the group speaking their names and each one stood up and said,

"I am happy to welcome you."

We replied,

"We are happy to know you."

The two thin dogs lay panting in the shade, while a rooster and chickens pecked the ground near them.

After lunch we exchanged gifts. The women had crocheted tablecloths, the children had woven baskets. We had brought books and toys for the younger children and transistor radios with a supply of batteries for the teenagers. It was Christmas in June.

Japhet brought out photograph albums. Most of his photos were of the Hochschild family - a record of them growing up, birthday parties, pool parties, posing with dogs and cats. Very few were of Japhet's family. He was absent for much of their lives.

Mike made a speech. He spoke of how much we loved Japhet and thanked the Zhanjes for sharing their father.

A shy young mother holding a toddler stood up and presented her three- year old,

"This is my Claudie," she said.

Tears flowed from many eyes as we said goodbye. The women stood at the side of the truck, singing a farewell song as we drove away.

After a mile or two Mike stopped the truck. We walked to a high point and waved, as the glowing red ball of sun disappeared, silhouetting the group still waving and singing.

The Xmas Party

The Johannesburg summer rainfall is in full spate in December, so it is decided the servants will have their annual Xmas party in the garage. With about forty people, including, spouses, friends and children, they do not want to take a chance of sitting in the garden and being rained out. We park our cars outside, tables and chairs are arranged in the garage even as a low rumble of thunder rolls across the highveld sky. It is raining hard as guests arrive. We hear laughter and music but suddenly Japhet Jhanje, my mother-in-law's cook, who has been with our family since he was a young man, and my husband a little boy, is now standing before us saying, "Mike, please come, we have trouble." Mike and two friends leave with Japhet. One is soon back to tell us the news. The party was in full swing, when suddenly the garage doors went up and they see a thief in my car, looking shocked at them looking at him. He must have hit the remote garage door opener, not knowing what it was. Remote control garage door openers were still in their infancy in Johannesburg, their function unknown to most. He leaps out of my car, dashes off on a bicycle, which we later learned he had stolen from our neighbors. An impi of irate Zulu partygoers give chase. Through the rain he pedals pursued by an angry mob. Through gardens, jumping over hedges, chasing him down roads, they set off a cacophony of barking dogs. Mike and his friend eventually come upon the group surrounding the thief. Thomas, Japhet's dapper elderly friend, who was standing on a corner, dressed, as always in his Sunday best (he had a job at the local bank) sees the thief peddling towards him. He sticks his umbrella through the spokes of the bike, the bike comes to a screeching halt, back tire lifts, throws the man over the handlebars much to the delight of the pursuing crowd. Mike calms the enraged guests while his friend calls the police.

The Flying Squad screeches to a stop, kicking up pebbles, two policemen jump out, pleased to be in action. Sam Sabinga, we learn his name later at the court trial, a habitual criminal, is sentenced to ten years in jail, no time off for good behavior. The guests return to their party, once again jubilant and a good time is had by all. Lenny, our nine year old son, has the last word about this incident. Months later when we explain to our children we are leaving South Africa, Lenny's face brightens after the initial shock and disappointment and he says, "You know, maybe it is a good thing we are going, because when Sam Sibinga gets out of jail and comes looking for us, we will be in America. He'll never find us there!

Family Secret

In 1978 the "brain drain" is in full swing, skilled professionals are emigrating for a number of reasons; Black consciousness has stirred discontent and been answered by more draconian laws; the previously white ruled neighboring countries of Mozambique and Angola have collapsed; whites see a dismal future; Apartheid is more firmly entrenched than ever; blacks see an equally dismal future.

Dad's brother and his wife, my aunt and uncle, are leaving South Africa, part of the continuing exodus. Their house is sold, air tickets booked, they are leaving in a few weeks.

My aunt brings a photograph to show my mother. "Look what I found at the back of a cupboard while I was clearing up yesterday."

Four young men and one pretty girl stare at the photographer.

"Who do you think the fourth man is?"

Mom recognizes Dad and his two brothers and sister.

"He has a strong family resemblance to the others," she replies.

"That's what I thought, but when I asked David, he told me he was a neighbor. I think my dear husband is hiding something."

I look at the sepia photograph. The people stand in a formal pose, staring at the photographer. I recognize my Dad's sister, his two brothers and Dad. The other man has a familial resemblance.

Mom shows the photograph to Dad that evening. He puts his head down; will not answer when she asks him about the fourth man. For the first time I see him crying in front of my mother. He will not talk.

I call cousins and we decide there is something hidden in our fathers' lives, and because they are not telling, it is up to us to unravel it. Weeks later a breakthrough; two cousins in Cape Town find a grave in an old cemetery. A brother, Hyman's existence hidden for years, now revealed. He died in the sixties, an elderly man, they have the birth and death dates. These facts do not answer the question why, but now the secret is revealed, Dad tells Mom about Hyman. The connection between the stranger in the photograph, which lay undiscovered for years in a dark cupboard, and Roy becomes clear. My father had another brother, Hyman, the fourth man. He was schizophrenic. They, an uncle and his nephew, both tipped out of life by lunacy and genetics. Hyman was institutionalized in Valkenberg Mental Hospital in Cape Town. He lived and died alone. The pact of secrecy was honored by his three brothers for years.

I am devastated by this news. Michael and I married in 1970, eight years before the secret was revealed. We discussed endlessly whether to have children or not, worried there might be a genetic connection between Roy's illness and any children of ours. We did not know if Roy's schizophrenia was genetically related. After much soul searching and being assured of sufficiently diluted blood lines, we had Claudie, eight in 1978 and Lenny, six. I implored my father to tell us how Hyman behaved, why it was kept a secret but after his initial confession to my mother, he would not speak. I was at a loss; furious, helpless, scared for the future of our children. And I was more resolved than ever Roy would not be hidden, that he would always know he is loved and never forgotten.

Emigrating

Steve Biko, the Black Consciousness leader died in prison in 1977, naked and manacled. When the Minister of Justice, Jimmy Kruger, was told, he responded, "It leaves me cold," we decided to leave the country and make a new home in the U.S.

We had been acting blind, deaf and dumb for too long. We lived through years of gross human rights violations. Many organizations, meetings and publications had been banned. "Black Beauty" was banned until it was realized it was the story of a horse! Activists had suffered teargas, whips, bullets, house arrests, tortures and death. Funerals became political rallies because political rallies were banned. Police raids flushed out people in humiliating, repetitive scenes. Their crime, being "illegal" (in places they were not allowed to be) according to information stamped in their Passbook - which Blacks had to carry at all times.

Apartheid was firmly entrenched. More vicious laws replaced previous ones, the police were all powerful. You defended apartheid, fought it or left if you could.

The goodbye "parties" were awful, I don't know how we moved through those days; walking for the last time out of the children's classrooms, through the school gates, trying to hold every detail in our minds, the smells, the feeling of the leaves, the sounds of the streets, saying goodbye to the neighborhood store owners, driving away from our house, which was no longer our house.

Saying goodbye to aging parents was heartbreaking; mine, stoic as ever, encouraged us to leave. We expected to see my mother-in-law as she was booked on a tour of New England and planned to stay with us, for a few weeks, at the end of the tour. Punchy, our black Labrador would be following on a later plane.

The huge plane began its ponderous taxiing down the runway, slowly lifting off into the African night sky. Through the blur of tears I saw the twinkling lights of Johannesburg below us, then behind us, tilting away as our world turned over.